Israel's Dead Soul

Israel's
Dead Soul

Steven Salaita

TEMPLE UNIVERSITY PRESS
Philadelphia

TEMPLE UNIVERSITY PRESS
Philadelphia, Pennsylvania 19122
www.temple.edu/tempress

Library of Congress Cataloging-in-Publication Data

Salaita, Steven, 1975-
  Israel's dead soul / Steven Salaita.
      p. cm.
  Includes bibliographical references and index.
  ISBN 978-1-4399-0637-8 (hardcover : alk. paper) —
  ISBN 978-1-4399-0638-5 (pbk. : alk. paper) —
  ISBN 978-1-4399-0639-2 (e-book)
  1. Israel and the diaspora. 2. Jews—Attitudes toward Israel. 3. Jews—
United States—Political activity. 4. National characteristics, Israeli.
5. Multiculturalism—Political aspects—Israel. 6. Politics and culture.
7. Israel—Ethnic relations. 8. Israel—Social conditions—21st century.
9. Israel—Politics and government—21st century. I. Title.
  DS134.S25 2011
  320.54095694—dc22
                          2010041459

Printed in the United States of America

2 4 6 8 9 7 5 3 1

For my mother, who taught me never to hate.
For my father, who taught me to hate injustice.

We all know that Art is not truth. Art is a lie that makes us realize the truth, at least the truth that is given to us to understand.

—Picasso

Contents

Acknowledgments

am immeasurably grateful for the living souls of my wonderful friends and colleagues. No book is created by an individual. They all grow out of tension and dialogue. *Israel's Dead Soul* is a product of intense and invigorating dialogue that has occurred and continues to occur with intelligent and compassionate people who are more than just names on a page to me.

For their superb feedback on parts or all of the manuscript, I would like to thank Piya Chatterjee, Sunaina Maira, and Houston Baker Jr. For their guidance and wisdom, I would like to thank Fred D'Aguiar, Virginia Fowler, J. Kēhaulani Kauanui, Magid Shihade, and Robert Warrior. For the inspiriting conversation, I would like to thank Mohammed Abed, Deborah Alkamano, Saher Safi, Matthew Shenoda, and Jessica Woodruff. For being the most efficient editor of all time, I would like to thank Micah Kleit. For being kick-ass family, I would like to thank Mom, Dad, Danya, and Michael. For the endless smiles they have provided, I would like to thank Eve and Nasr.

And for being everything that I could ever possibly hope to be, I would like to thank Diana, my political muse, most demanding reader, and comeliest sparring partner.

Israel's Dead Soul

Introduction

srael's soul has been the subject of much anguish. Writers and politicians have been lamenting its demise for decades. Shalem Center senior fellow Daniel Gordis believes that policy should invoke "something incredibly powerful and positive about the Israeli soul."[1] For decades, novelist David Grossman complains, settlers "have operated in the gray areas of the Jewish-Israeli soul."[2] He also claims that "the agonized Israeli soul, hardened by external and internal wars, is . . . ardent about finally divesting itself of the burden of constant animosity."[3] Richard Silverstein, of the liberal blog *Tikun Olam*, abhors the murder of donkeys and other animals by the Israeli occupation forces (IOF). "This is what the Occupation does to the Israeli soul," he laments. "It kills it in the most mundane of ways."[4] Israel's soul is even the subject of an entire book by Yoram Hazony, *The Jewish State: The Struggle for Israel's Soul*. In it he notes that Israel represents "the regions of the soul that must continue to glow and shimmer and dance if the Jewish state is to live."[5]

Writer Yigal Schwartz is more theatrical, proclaiming, "There's something in the Israeli soul that makes it resist entering a state of normalcy. I sound like a prophet, but that's my feeling."[6] It is presumably the incomprehensible mechanisms of this fastidious soul and not economic or ideological factors that have prevented Israel from achieving peace. Jewish Voice for Peace activist Tsela

Barr mourns that Israel's occupation "has, in the words of one rabbi, 'morally corrupted the Israeli soul.'"[7] Israel's soul even has its own corporeal identity; Yehuda Amichai, who died in 2000, was recently honored with the distinction of being dubbed the "poet of Israel's soul."[8] Daily newspaper *Yediot Aharonot* calls humanitarian activist Gal Lusky an "Israeli soul commando."[9] Israel's soul has been searched so frequently and thoroughly that it must be remarkably elusive to have thus far avoided offering pithily wise life lessons to its many interlocutors. It is not the discovery of answers that counts, however; it is the search itself into the soul that portends moral decency. Israel, after all, faces a soul-searching double standard, according to Cathy Young, for "this self-questioning is an important process essential to a democratic society. But it also highlights the rather appalling double standard in the world's response."[10] On the other hand, "The very question of whether similar soul-searching is being done by Hamas, the Palestinian terrorist organization which is also the elected leadership of Gaza, would be darkly funny."[11]

The formulation is clear: soul-searching is an act of modernity; not doing so intimates a barbarism of deeply immoral origin. Worrying over the state of Israel's soul, then, is the apogee of a civilized mind. Such worrying does not portend Israel's decline; it reaffirms Israel's fortitude. If Israel's citizens didn't fret over its soul then Israel would be no better than an Arab state—it would have no reason to exist. It is a lesson journalist Antony Loewenstein understands, noting that "if Israel is to survive for another 60 years, it will need to understand that the ongoing occupation has corrupted its soul."[12] Soul-searching and Israel's survival are coterminous matters. This burden can be a full-time job. After all, as Yossi Klein Halevi points out, "No country's soul has been more severely tested than Israel's."[13]

This book is not about the decline or death of Israel's soul. It is about the proliferation of anguished speculation about the decline or death of Israel's soul. Israel's soul is so significant that it was the subject of a BBC event entitled "Is Israel Losing Its Soul?" To my knowledge, no other country has had its soul publicly examined by a panel of experts. All nations throughout history have been endowed with souls by zealous or anxious citizens, but Israel is unique insofar as its soul is under constant scrutiny. There are many reasons for this scrutiny, but it largely can be attributed to two factors: (1) Israel's self-image as exceptional requires a fair amount of idealistic anguish, and (2) Israel's moral and legal misdeeds necessitate a professed commitment to self-improvement based on the nostalgia of an invented past. Analyzing the multitudinous examinations of Israel's soul is the best way to undertake a study of Zionist cultural and political expression, for it is the invented soul of the national entity, Israel, in which emotional and intellectual relationships are housed. Those who praise or lament Israel's soul are actually telling us about various ethical perspectives for which the soul is merely a fanciful metonym. Nobody has ever mourned the condition of Israel's soul without being deeply attached to Israel as an ethnocentric state.

A specific motif arises from this commitment and becomes evident in Zionist art, scholarship, and activism. Much Zionist discourse expresses a yearning for the simpler innocence of an idealized Jewish liberation, one undiluted by the barbarity of conflict with Palestinians. This yearning, like all forms of ethnonationalism, relies on nostalgia and historical cherry-picking, but it is especially persistent in phenomena in some way trained on Israel. Zionism presents its advocates with irreconcilable contradictions. It promises liberation through colonization. It attempts to exemplify modernity but relies on a fundamentally tribal mentality. It glorifies democracy while practicing apartheid. There is no way to circumvent these realities; one cannot support Zionism without eventually encountering its ugly side. As a result, specific discursive strategies arise, and those strategies pervade all forms of Zionist celebration and introspection.

This book explores those strategies, paying close attention to how scrutiny of the soul of Israel portends a broader attempt to normatize—that is, to render normative—Zionism as a benign ideology of polite multicultural conviviality. This ideology and liberal American discourses of multiculturalism are profoundly intertwined. The following chapters assess various modes of Zionist self-expression—scholarly, filmic, activist, philosophical—to illuminate how Zionism's advocates have successfully integrated the ideology into popular notions of enlightenment and political decency. To contest the conflation of Zionism and liberal multiculturalism presents great challenges. There is a danger that we will treat liberal multiculturalism as a panacea into which Zionism unjustifiably imposes itself. In reality, the two phenomena are so readily conflated because they represent the same ersatz righteousness, arising from the same unexamined ubiquity of colonization and structural power imbalance. I am interested in teasing out some of the ways that Zionism has become a vital component of the liberal discourses of inclusiveness, coexistence, and multiculturalism that have been attacked as inadequate from the political left and from scholars working in indigenous, postcolonial, and critical race studies. I extend these critiques, but with emphasis on an as-yet attenuated discussion of how ethnic cleansing has come to be tacitly acceptable through lionization of Zionism and multiculturalism in liberal discourses of American modernity.

This task requires some definitional precision in the face of disputed and capacious terminology. The terms "multiculturalism" and "Zionism" merit a specific usage. No matter what definition I proffer, it will be incomplete and contestable. My goal is not to provide a comprehensive definition, as such an outcome is impossible; my goal instead is to provide a definition that denotes a specific usage representing a discernible politics, morality, and worldview. Even this goal is dubious, but it is the most realistic way to critique palpable issues of theoretical, political, and cultural import. We must remember that Zionism, as difficult as it is to define, is an ideology that supports a colossal military enterprise and underlies one of the greatest and most intractable conflicts of our time. Multiculturalism is similarly multivalent but no less important, for it directly affects policy not only at the level of bureaucratic protocol but also at crucial sites of capitalist power.

I do not want to simplify Zionism in this book but do believe it is possible to reduce it to some basic commitments. In my usage, which I have derived from analysis of numerous political discourses, "Zionism" is in essence and practice the belief that Jews have the right to a nation-state in historic Palestine that is majority Jewish. The creation of Israel in 1948 is therefore justified despite the ugliness that accompanied its formation. From this central belief, Zionists diverge into numerous sociopolitical attitudes, many of them at great odds with one another. Some are adamantly opposed to Israel's military occupation of the West Bank, Gaza Strip, and Golan Heights; others believe in Israel's divine right to expel Palestinian Arabs from those territories and replace them with Jews. It is because of these divergent attitudes that Zionism appears so complex or even ambivalent. However, in its patronage of a Jewish state it is remarkably uncomplicated, and I have little concern for its disjunctions beyond this elementary attribute. In the tradition of Hannah Arendt, Edward Said, Martin Buber, Malcolm X, and a host of other seminal thinkers, I conceptualize Zionism as deeply inhumane ethically, and as destructive politically, for Jews and Arabs, and for humankind in general.

My ethical and political reasoning will become clear as this book progresses, but it might be useful to offer an introductory comment about my opposition to Zionism. It is not an opposition that exists in overzealous isolation; it is rather a vital component of an integrated moral worldview that deplores all forms of legal imbalance based on ethnicity, religion, gender, or any other cultural factor. Israel's history, like the ideology of Zionism that preceded it, has been complex in the way that all national histories are complex, but its most consistent feature has been that of exclusion. When Zionism started as a political movement in the late nineteenth century, Palestine was overwhelmingly Arab, with a Muslim majority and a significant Christian minority along with smaller communities of Jews, Druze, and European transplants. European Jews gradually began settling Palestine, often buying land from absentee landlords in Beirut, much to the surprise and displeasure of Palestinian farmers and merchants. As the Jewish population in Palestine increased, clashes between the settlers and the native Palestinians ensued, with the British, the colonial power of the time, seeking to assuage Arab displeasure while laying the foundation for the emergence of a Jewish state.

On the eve of Israel's creation in 1948, Palestine was majority Arab and the majority of its land was Arab owned. However, in 1947 the United Nations proposed a plan to partition Palestine that would have offered the Palestinians 46 percent of historic Palestine, much of it nonarable. The Arabs rejected the offer. Israel subsequently seized 78 percent of historic Palestine, in the process displacing approximately seven hundred thousand Palestinians and committing a series of massacres in Deir Yassin, Tartura, Beit Daras, and other villages. In 1967 Israel captured the West Bank, Gaza Strip, Golan Heights (Syria), and Sinai Peninsula (Egypt), creating over two hundred thousand more Palestinian refugees and deploying napalm on the fleeing civilians. Israel subsequently returned Sinai to Egypt, but retains control of the West Bank and has annexed the Golan Heights. Israel removed Jewish settlers from the Gaza Strip but retains tight control over the territory, subjecting its 1.5 million residents to crippling and deadly economic sanctions.[14]

The Israel-Palestine conflict is largely territorial. Israel occupies the West Bank militarily and has employed a settlement policy there resulting in a disparate set of laws for Jews and Palestinians. Jewish settlers, numbering around four hundred thousand, have access to highways, land, and territory from which Palestinians are excluded. Inside Israel, the Palestinians comprise approximately 20 percent of the population. They too are subject to institutionalized discrimination in the areas of housing, movement, and employment. This community, which effectively occupies a second-class status, also experiences calls for forcible deportation by politicians and religious demagogues.[15] Zionism, the ideology that underlies Israel, calls for a privileging of Jews, a commitment that is evident at all levels of Israeli society. Archbishop Desmond Tutu has described Israel's behavior toward Palestinians as comparable to apartheid South Africa.[16] Former president Jimmy Carter has suggested that Israel's behavior is worse than that of apartheid South Africa.[17] I do not use the terms "ethnic cleansing," "colonization," or "ethnonationalism" as hyperbole or belittlement, then. I use them as accurate legal and moral descriptors of Israel's behavior in the past and present.

I cannot deny the seminal role the Israel-Palestine conflict has played in my personal and professional life, but I would point out that rejecting Zionism is not a singling out of Israel for special criticism, as supporters of Israel often assert. Even if one singles out Israel for criticism, a prospect that makes little temporal sense, it does not mean that the criticism is aberrant or exceptional. Nor does it automatically absolve Israel of the unsavory actions for which it is so often criticized despite the hope of its supporters that accusing critics of singling out Israel will amount to an act of involuntary absolution. I offer this point to acknowledge that, although I am not singling out Israel in this book, I am focusing on it with ardent determination and have no interest in absolving Israel or any other state either voluntarily or involuntarily. My analysis arises from a careful exploration of multitudinous sources and a rigid adherence to internationally established standards of human rights and moral behavior in times of conflict.

I reject Zionism in both its secular and religious manifestations for two main reasons: because it arises from and practices juridical segregation based on a cardinal element of biological determinism (that Jews should have access to a special set of rights from which Palestinians are excluded for no other reason than their non-Jewishness), and because I support the profuse movements for sovereignty and independence undertaken by global indigenous communities who are still subject to various forms of colonization. The Palestinians are one of many national groups seeking to practice self-determination on an autonomous ancestral land base. Because of its close relationship with the United States and its extensive neoliberal commitments, assessment of Israel is central to global campaigns for economic, racial, sexual, and environmental justice. Zionism is indubitably on the side of capitalist and colonialist power, a fact demonstrated by nearly every relevant Israeli policy decision since its creation. Neoconservative George Gilder amusingly illustrates it in his 2009 book, *The Israel Test*,[18] which argues that one's level of support for Israel accurately portends commitment to capitalism, American military prowess, and the war on terror. Gilder conceptualizes these benchmarks as necessary dimensions of the responsible citizen, but his argument, which accurately posits that a neoconservative outlook and Israel are coterminous, must surely be devastating to those who fancy themselves both Zionist and progressive.

In a more philosophical capacity, numerous scholars have pointed to the inherent problems with directing personal support to states and their bureaucratic institutions.[19] These problems constitute another reason for wariness about Zionism, which relies on a liberatory structure premised on a nation-state model that the countries in Europe from which it emerged now conceptualize as antiquated. Nation-state models of communal organization inevitably exclude segments of the population, a problem that in Israel is overwhelmingly acute. It is important to think about justice in an extragovernmental capacity, relying not on state bureaucracies but on the power of democratic communities to create inclusive and sustainable social systems. To support Zionism is to place belief in the probity of the state, a dubious proposition, and in a myth of democracy that is inherently exclusionary. It is outside the purview of the modern nation-state that Arabs and Jews most fruitfully coexisted; it is directly from the ideological deficiencies of the modern nation-state that the Nazi Holocaust occurred.

As to the counterpart of Zionism in this book, multiculturalism, it is less loaded politically but more ambivalent terminologically, its main pratfall. I deploy the term throughout this book to identify a policy more than an ideology. By "policy," I refer to legal or administrative mandates that inform corporate, governmental, or educational protocol, whereas "ideology" refers to an idea, sometimes abstract, that provides a site of critical analysis. There is little reason to connect multiculturalism to ideology unless we deploy some of the magisterial notions of ideology. Its origin is in human resources management for corporate demography. From there, it has pervaded university, nonprofit, activist, and educational protocol. It is now part of the everyday vocabulary of the vast majority of American workplaces, community organizations, and entertainment venues. I'm most interested not in what multiculturalism promises, which is an inclusive space free of discrimination and accepting of diverse cultures, but in what it ignores. The language of justice and reparation is almost completely absent from multiculturalist discourses; despite the notorious ambiguity of these terms, their exclusion denotes an unmistakable refusal to engage the problems the terms underline. Discussion of racism is likewise rare in multiculturalist discourses and tends to be cursory and decontextualized from foreign policy and economics where it does exist. It is these modes of multicultural devotion that are of concern in this book. They emerge from liberal traditions of Western modernity and thus are usually at odds with both critical race and decolonial theory. I critique multiculturalism with the goal of illustrating why it has been so easy for Israel's supporters to inscribe Zionist ideology into its vocabulary and praxis.

This amalgamation of Zionism and multiculturalism results in a number of surprisingly underexamined phenomena of concern to scholars and activists. This book is concerned mainly with three of those phenomena: (1) Immersing Israel in the philosophical and discursive context of multicultural humanism allows that humanism to be invoked as a rationale for responsible and progressive support of Israel, making it disreputable to condemn Israel for anything more than excess and to criticize Zionism at all. The conjoining of humanism and Zionism is actualized through constant reference to Israel's credentials for modernity such as democracy, gay rights, and secularism. (2) As something of an extension of the previous point, but distinct enough to warrant its own close assessment, I explore how scholars and artists have constantly reproduced the formulations that conflate Zionism with multicultural humanism. This exploration is most relevant in light of my argument that some Zionist civil rights organizations, the Anti-Defamation League (ADL) most notably, can be accurately classified as hate groups. (3) Many of the moral problems I identify in the following chapters arise from the systematic conflation by Zionists (and others) of Jews and Israel. Such a conflation is dangerous for many reasons. It is dangerous to Jews because it forces even the unwilling into an ethnonationalist stance. It is even more dangerous to Palestinians because it excludes them legally and historically from the physical and emotional spaces of their very constitution as a discrete national community. More specifically, the conflation of Jews and Israel relies on a host of unsustainable assumptions and dubious colonial mythologies.

All of these matters inform the status of Israel's soul, the venerable barometer of Israel's reputation around the world. The need to normatize Israel as a participant in the civilities of modernity increases as Israel is criticized for the ruthlessness of its colonial policies. In turn, the desire increases among Zionists to elide colonization by transforming Israel into a timeless democracy central to the promise of American multiculturalism. This sort of move happens in multitudinous ways, in variegated circumstances. *Israel's Dead Soul* explores some of these discursive and political moves, illustrating the surprising ways Zionism has become integral to the very notions of modernity and multiculturalism.

Chapter 1, "Israel as Cultural Icon: The Vacillating Boundaries of Jewish Identity," assesses the profound joining of Jewishness with Israel, paying special note to how the ethos of multiculturalism facilitate that juxtaposition. Chapter 2, "Is the Anti-Defamation League a Hate Group?" answers the question through a close reading of the ADL's imperatives and activities, invoking the ADL's own criteria for a hate group to identify some shocking affinities. Chapter 3, "Ethnonationalism as an Object of Multicultural Decorum: The Case of Cornel West and Michael Eric Dyson," examines the scholarly and popular work of West and Dyson to show how the pratfalls of multiculturalist discourse limit useful analysis of the race, class, and power dynamics with which their work is concerned. While it might surprise readers to see West and Dyson featured in a book that critiques Zionism, Chapter 3 makes it clear why they are appropriate inclusions. Chapter 4, "Sexuality, Violence, and Modernity in Israel: The Paradise of Not Being Arab," surveys and criticizes the recent initiatives that Zionist organizations, in conjunction with Israel's government, have developed to invoke gay rights as the defining metonym of Israeli civility, as against the emblematic barbarism of Arab and Muslim homophobia. Chapter 5, "The Heart of Darkness Redux, Again," discusses a number of films that either tacitly or lucidly reproduce Joseph Conrad's archetypal dark heart motif through representation of an inherent inhumanity deep within Zionism brought out by the Jewish encounter with Palestinians.

In closing, I would like to say a few words about the title. I have chosen it not to be cheeky or provocative but to highlight two points central to my argument. First, discussion of the state of Israel's soul has been common for so long that it constitutes a relevant political and moral discourse on its own, one that illuminates numerous important features of Zionist identity and strategy. Those who chatter about Israel's declining soul long ago killed it by agonizing it to death. However, in so doing they have brought other matters to life, most notably a commitment to protecting Israel from recognition of its inherent iniquities, which I endeavor to contextualize here. Second, I am working from the belief that Israel's soul died in the moment of its invention. I do not believe states have souls, metaphysically or metaphorically. There is no soul of Palestine, of Iraq, of Papua New Guinea, of Canada, or of any other geopolitical entity with a central government and an economic apparatus.

Israel is the least likely of nations to have a soul, given its creation through ethnic cleansing and its current policies of garrison colonization. The idea of a national soul arises from the metonymical fantasy that there is an innate good in the national community encapsulated by the state, that the natural progression of a nation-state is toward fulfilling a promise of fundamental goodness. The soul is the state's guardian, keeping the inadvertent badness of governance in check so the inherent goodness of national ideals can be fulfilled. There is no evidence to substantiate any belief that the goal of a nation-state is to do good. Nation-states, like corporations, exist to enrich those who fortify their power. The fantasies of goodness proffered by the soul-searchers, then, substitute the entire populace of the nation-state for its economic and political elite. The other main problem with the notion of a national soul is that no nation-state adequately embodies its entire population; a minority community (or, more likely, various minority communities) is always excluded from the normative national identity. In the case of Israel, all non-Jews are aliens or challenges to the soul of the nation.

Meditation on Israel's anguished soul, close analysis illustrates, is mostly an excuse to consciously ignore its violence or to disregard the structural qualities of that violence. This reality is visible in a plethora of Zionist politics and cultures, as we shall see in the chapters that follow. My goal in this book is to carefully analyze how these politics and cultures illuminate some telling characterizations of the state of Zionism today. My hope is that readers will let lie Israel's dead soul and examine Israel's destruction of actual minds and bodies instead.

1 Israel as Cultural Icon

The Vacillating Boundaries of Jewish Identity

> Lies are often much more plausible, more appealing
> to reason, than reality, since the liar has the great
> advantage of knowing beforehand what the audience
> wishes or expects to hear.
>
> —HANNAH ARENDT, CRISES OF THE REPUBLIC (1972)

On an ordinary day in the spring of 2008, I was navigating throngs of thirsty and hungry students between classes at Virginia Tech's Squires Student Center, in pursuit of a watery but much-needed cup of coffee. After emerging from the energetic and impatient crowd, I saw that I had a bit of time before my next class and decided to drop by the multicultural student office down the hall so I could chat with its director, a friendly and intelligent man. My friend wasn't in the office, but the trip nevertheless ended up being instructive. Adorning the modestly sized anteroom of the multicultural center were dozens of Israeli flags in various sizes, covering nearly every visible surface of the room, along with pamphlets extolling Israel's exceptionalness or decrying its poor reputation and continually embattled status. It turned out it was Jewish Awareness Month at Virginia Tech, but I had difficulty understanding what awareness of Jewish culture has to do with puffery of a nation-state and recapitulation of its propaganda. I had even more difficulty understanding why the promotion of Israel would be housed in an office devoted at least nominally to intercultural understanding and the elimination of racism. My goal in this chapter is to use systematic cultural and political analysis to make some sense of these phenomena, particularly the ways that Israel and Jewish culture are conflated to varying ends and with varying levels of sincerity.

I should make clear that I'm skeptical of the utility of any multicultural office in a university setting as an agent of justice. There are many reasons for this skepticism. The primary one is an understanding that most offices of multicultural affairs are entrenched institutionally and therefore beholden to institutions, not to the people most in need of intervention (minority students, poor students, underpaid support staff, landscapers and janitors, and so forth). I also find problems with many of the philosophical and political manifestations of multiculturalism as an attitude and a prescription for social interaction. These are matters I examine later in this chapter and throughout this book. I add a qualification here: although I am pessimistic about the possibilities of extant multicultural discourses as an antidote to racism, I am not at all opposed to the creation of spaces under the rubric of multiculturalism where students and staff can hang out, hold events, and create educational programs. Such spaces are useful and necessary. I simply don't see them as transformative structurally vis-à-vis the institutions in which they are housed. There are other ways to think about the effective contestation of racism and the constructive exchange of cultural practices; I consider some of these other ways in my analysis of the political uses of cultural identity.

As to Virginia Tech's multicultural office, I was disturbed to see what for many students are symbols of ethnic cleansing festooned all over one of the designated safe spaces on campus. (The "safe space" is another liberal concept I find troublesome. Does its existence mean that hate is justified everywhere else? Or that discomfort is verboten?) I wasn't terribly surprised, though, because I know that on college campuses support of Israel is a prerequisite of responsible multicultural citizenship. The director of the multicultural office probably doesn't have strong feelings about the Israel-Palestine conflict (I am venturing a guess here; despite our friendship, it's not something we've ever discussed). And he would never consciously be party to an act of cultural insensitivity. His willingness to display a controversial symbol in an office dedicated to students of color simply reflects the success Zionists have had in marketing Israel as a quixotic experiment appropriate for multicultural celebration. Israel is a natural outcome of multicultural consciousness, according to many Zionists, and so it is perfectly normal to include (or privilege) it in proud displays of diversity.

I considered telling my friend that the display of Israel's flag is inappropriate because for some it signifies hostility and because celebration of a settler-colonial state shouldn't fall under the purview of a multicultural office (or any institution with moral decency). I ultimately demurred, however, for a few reasons: it is not my business to tell another person how to run his office; the level of Zionist entrenchment on our campus is such that it would take a superhuman effort to dislodge it; and a superhuman effort to dislodge Zionism from a multicultural office is not the best place to direct our energy, because even if such a move were to be successful, it's not always the most fruitful site of contestation. I would like to dislodge Zionism from political systems instead.

These aren't easy goals to work out. They are accompanied by a variety of ethical and strategic complexities that demand careful analysis. This chapter undertakes that sort of analysis, which I extend throughout the remainder of the book. In particular, I examine the relationship between discourses of multiculturalism and celebration of Israel. This relationship is most frequently cultivated in the context of liberal democratic notions of progress and modernity. As enlightened as advocates of these notions fancy themselves, they are ideas in fact deeply connected to the colonial epistemologies of an era that never quite achieves the status of bygone.

The Problems of Synchronous Politics and Culture

Much of the so-called culture wars of the past decade have focused on perceptions of the Middle East and the accusations of antiSemitism that frequently accompany criticism of Israel. A number of books have been published in recent years either affirming or challenging the conflation of anti-Semitism and criticism of Israel.[1] Most of these books discuss the technical and moral dimensions of anti-Semitism and apply these discussions to particular conceptions of Israel's ethnic character and military behavior. There has not been enough close reading of the rhetorical and discursive features of the conflation of anti-Semitism and criticism of Israel. We must think about the conditions in which Israel supposedly inspires anti-Semitism. The conflation in question is framed mainly by the popular construction of Israel as a state coterminous with an ethnic group. Most of Israel's supporters are adamant that Israel is a state for all Jews, and thus an entity that cannot be detached from ethnicity. This condition is common to most nation-states, but in the case of Israel the juxtaposition of national belonging and ethnic background is explicit juridically and rhetorically. It is not Israel's enemies but its advocates who juxtapose Israeli citizenship and Jewish identity. In other words, if it is true that Israel evokes anti-Semitism, then according to their own logic it is primarily the fault of Israel's most passionate supporters.

It is not my goal to assign the blame for the existence of anti-Semitism to anybody. Racism, a category in which anti-Semitism belongs, is a complex phenomenon, dynamic and multivalent. The blame for racism ultimately rests in the existence of injustice from which individuals or groups benefit economically, psychologically, or politically. Individuals, governments, and corporations also play a prominent role in its survival. I want to be clear that I am not blaming anti-Semitism on Jews, then. I am, however, making the crucial distinction between the existence of anti-Semitism as a historical affliction and the ardent defense of Israel as necessarily Jewish and how that sort of discourse facilitates its dissemination. More important, that sort of discourse places a type of onus on Israel that its supporters would surely consider unsavory, which is to act as an emissary for Jews throughout the world. In defending Israel's eternal and inherent Jewish nature, its supporters have no choice but to reinforce that onus. This defense isn't so much a Faustian bargain as it is a starkly utilitarian choice that has far-reaching consequences for the many people whose lives are affected by Israel's comportment and identity.

An especially rich site of discovery for the coagulation of Jewish and Israeli identity is the college campus, where societal debates often convene in microcosmic form. The colonization of Virginia Tech's multicultural office by Zionists is a manifestation of a certain politics that many Jewish organizations cultivate. Virginia Tech's Jewish community, usually through the sponsorship of Hillel and Friends of Israel at the university, hosts an annual Jewish Awareness Month every spring in conjunction with the office of Multicultural Programs and Services, which assists all student groups with cultural awareness celebrations.

I like the idea of a Jewish Awareness Month. As a college student I participated eagerly in programs of awareness of Arab cultures (and politics, though the groups with which I worked were careful to separate the two as much as possible). We even gave our events silly titles like Palestine Awareness Week, Arabian Nights, and Arab Awareness Month, the kinds of program names that are campus standards. Helping to organize these events played a huge role in my intellectual development; I am a proponent of student involvement in political causes and cultural celebrations. I encourage my students at Virginia Tech to participate in the various extracurricular initiatives on campus. Much of the programming associated with Jewish Awareness Month at Virginia Tech effectively illuminates both serious and lighthearted elements of Jewish culture to non-Jewish audiences. Thus it plays an important role in the cultural interchange that is supposed to occur on a college campus. This cultural interchange isn't all hugs and smiles, though. It often takes place in contested arenas; the contestations frequently occur around race and religion. Despite the lack of empirical evidence, I would guess that conflicts between Jewish and Arab student groups are the most common these days. Moreover, the act of sharing a cultural tradition or expression is never neutral. The act inevitably entails a version or interpretation of cultural practice, often representative of a majority population, that is at least implicitly determined by politics.

Celebration of Jewish culture in the United States frequently is inseparable from political support of Israel. This style of celebration represents a particular version of cultural practice but appears to be the predominant mode of exhibiting Jewishness in rehearsed settings. Virginia Tech's 2008 Jewish Awareness Month, for example, had eighteen listed events. Of these eighteen events, six promoted Israel. The 2009 Jewish Awareness Month featured ten events devoted in some way to Israel. Zionism is a normative dimension of Jewishness in this schema. I collected information about other Jewish culture groups around the country, and it shows that Virginia Tech's is not an anomaly. The College of New Jersey Hillel features an Israel festival. The University of Oklahoma has an Israel festival with big-name speakers, including one year the state's governor. Duke University's Jewish Awareness Week includes an Israel Day, displayed prominently in the week's advertisement, featuring a hookah and what is supposed to be Israeli food (hummus and pita bread). Many of these Jewish Awareness celebrations are remarkably similar in content and political outlook. They also employ comparable promotional strategies, which can best be described as an attempt to sound as hip and apolitical as possible. Duke's graphic shows Stars of David in the manner of Caribbean vacation advertisements and promises "cool Israeli T-Shirts."

Virginia Tech's 2008 Jewish Awareness Month kicked up the hip factor even more, titling the proceedings "Judaism Y'all: Beyond Dreidels and Bagels." The month featured an ongoing "Best Bar Mitzvah Day Ever," along with a "Gay Shabbat" and a "Chocolate Seder." The program didn't actually get too far beyond the dreidel or the bagel, but it did find room for the preparation of "traditional Israeli" food such as couscous and hummus. The events at Duke and Virginia Tech are exemplary of the types of programs sponsored by Hillel across the country: they feature fun-loving portrayals of Jewish culture blended with ostensibly hip (but invariably tacky) promotion of Israel as chic and convivial. The apolitical presentation of Israel belies the implicitly politicized nature of the programming. It is a highly tendentious act to conceptualize Israel as timeless and normative, as if it has always been where Palestine once stood. It requires moxie and overconfidence to ignore the brutal colonial war it has long been waging. Then there is the shameless pilferage of Palestinian cuisine, among dozens of other appropriations (music, *argeela*, dress); these infidelities include the standard (and hopelessly clunky) white appropriation of black cultural expression. The Duke Friends of Israel logo even deftly includes all of Palestine in its silhouette of Israel.

These tendentious acts aren't necessarily orchestrated, but they are interconnected. Hillel is almost always involved in the promotion of Israel on campus either as a sponsor or an organizer. Hillel is headquartered in Washington, D.C., and has a presence on every major campus in the United States. A close reading of its educational materials illustrates that it is deeply committed to Israel and eager to promote the state as a beacon of modernity through slick promotional campaigns. Criticism of Israel is verboten in Hillel discourse. The organization has been working hard since the emergence of pro-Palestine voices to prepare its local chapters for what it conceptualizes as an onslaught of perplexing and aggressive opposition. It is also invested in marketing strategies for Israel that ignore its military occupation of the West Bank and emphasize instead its wealth of American-style modernity. Hillel doesn't treat the Israel-Palestine conflict as a solvable dispute that requires dialogue and a just resolution. It approaches the conflict as a propaganda contest in which Israel must be defended as a matter of principle. Hillel's depoliticization of Israel's colonial mandate facilitates its marketing strategy. When groups opposed to Israel's policy criticize the state, Hillel relies on a decontextualized victimology, one that evokes the Holocaust and anti-Semitism without mentioning Jewish violence in Israel, to reframe the issue from one of colonization to one of unfair persecution. Because Israel is inscribed in the daily observance of Jewish culture, to criticize it is to simultaneously perform an attack against the Jewish people. This logic underlies Hillel's claims to multicultural belonging.

In campus promotions, Israel is usually described as follows:

- A land that's fun and effervescent
- A fabulous place for study abroad
- A great opportunity for American Jews to connect to their culture
- A promised land of multicultural splendor, representing Jews from over fifty countries
- A thriving democracy surrounded by hostile, undemocratic enemies
- An exotic nation housing an uninterrupted ancient culture
- A place with a punchy, unlikely origin as a David against intractable Arab Goliaths
- The exclusive territory of Jews from around the world

The most noteworthy facet of these representations of Israel is not what they describe, but what they omit. There is rarely mention of Arabs or Palestinians as anything other than existential threats to Israel. There is never acknowledgment of Israel's military occupation or even of its colonial origin; Israel is invented as a timeless entity liberated from the tyranny of Great Britain and the obstructionism of the Arabs. These portrayals represent more than just putting a good foot forward. They arise from a meticulous campaign to market Israel on college campuses as a modern antidote to the barbarity of the Arabs and their dubious supporters.

Hillel, which operates on a budget of more than $40 million, devotes much of its attention to Israel's image.[2] The organization bills itself as a gathering space for Jewish students and a civic advocate of Jewish culture, but its purview is not limited to innocuous community-building activities. It makes a concerted effort to prepare students for conflict with those it deems hostile to Israel. It also supports Israel from the radically conventional perspective of its state policy justifications. An analysis of Hillel's Summit 2008, "Imagining a More Civil Society: The University and the Jewish Community," shows the organization to be paradoxically slavish but pugnacious. The gathering featured the usual cadre of heavy hitters, from Hillel brass like Edgar Bronfman and Wayne Firestone to numerous university deans and presidents. The introductory letters to the conference feature the vague platitudes typical of overproduced or corporate functions (e.g., "We'll develop the skills to promote civility, acceptance, and conflict resolution"; "As we imagine a more civil society, we will focus deeply on discourse itself and also on activities that foster safe dialogue and productive contributions to society"; "We will demonstrate what we hope to lead on campus: respectful, authentic conversations in which we hold multiple truths simultaneously, listening carefully while articulating our own thoughts and opening ourselves to letting go and learning anew").[3] These are sentiments befitting a summit complete with a green consciousness, whose packet boasts that only fair-trade coffee will be served and leftover food will be donated to D.C. Central Kitchen. The production resembles a Young Democrats conference with an ethnic twist.

Nowhere in the packet's front matter is there mention of Israel. The great majority of presentations likewise avoid the topic, concentrating instead on such topics as philanthropy, dialogue, technology, diversity, and service learning. The only geographical space identified in the program is Darfur, the darling issue of organized Jewish activism. Yet Hillel's devotion to Israel is no secret; an entire section of its website is reserved for promotion of Israel as a destination for students and a nation worthy of unqualified support. Hillel proclaims that "Israel touches on dimensions of collective and national Jewish identity and is intrinsically linked to Jewish Peoplehood."[4] Israel, Hillel continues, "as a multi-dimensional, dynamic and constantly evolving idea and reality provides a flexible and rich set of entry points into Jewishness, Jewish identity and Jewish community for our students."[5] Hillel greatly emphasizes study abroad and birthright programs, reflecting the deep desire of Zionists to outfit Israel with a normative status. Taglit-Birthright Israel seems to be a typical travel opportunity for students, but it is terribly disquieting upon inspection. It is reserved only for Jewish students, which is a huge problem morally and politically: American Jews are not indigenous to Israel but other people are—the unmentioned Palestinians who are excluded from these trips and in most cases from Israel altogether. Moreover, the very notion of a birthright vis-à-vis a geopolitical entity contravenes every possible articulation of liberal humanism or democratic citizenship. Hillel even constricts eligibility for Taglit-Birthright to non-Israeli Jews who haven't lived in Israel past the age of twelve. This reinforces its firm juxtaposition of Israel, a manifest nation-state, with deterritorialized Jews who have a genealogical claim to the symbolic, exclusive space Israel represents.

Is there a connection between Hillel's eschewal of Israel at its summit and its enthusiastic advocacy of Israel on campus? It may appear that any connection between these apparently divergent strategies would be only tenuous, but in fact there is an important connection that allows us to better understand the discourses of Jewish nationhood as they relate to the state of Israel. Hillel endeavors to do two things generally: encourage civic responsibility and promote the state of Israel. In Hillel's moral schema, these two goals are not exclusive, but aligned. This occurrence of synchronous politics and culture has devastating consequences. By proclaiming that being a good citizen includes supporting Israel, Hillel renders ethnonationalism a central element of civic responsibility. Its philosophy is ethnonationalist because it reserves access to a specific national land for only one ethnic group at the direct expense of other groups with greater claim to that land morally and historically. Hillel's policy statement on Israel makes this position clear: "Hillel is steadfastly committed to the support of Israel as Jewish and Democratic State with secure and recognized borders and as a member of the family of free nations."[6]

Because Israel has over a million Palestinian citizens who suffer institutional discrimination and rules over 4.5 million other Palestinians in the Occupied Territories who have no civil rights,

Hillel's collation of Judeocentrism and democracy is empirically untrue. Even the idea of Israel itself as a Jewish state is more mythology than reality. In making this assertion, I draw a distinction between Israel as it has been invented in Zionist discourses of Jewish ownership and the actual nation-state that has long been conflicted over its secular self-image and its perpetually crisis-stricken ethnocentric demography. The marketing of Israel is quite different from its existential realities, which often reveal ugly behavior that arises inevitably from a situation in which ethnic origin dictates belonging and citizenship. There is only so much bragging about democracy that a nation can do when it prevents an indigenous population from accessing even the most basic rights of citizenship. When I made the claim that the juxtaposition of civic responsibility and support of Israel has devastating consequences, I did not intend it to be hyperbolic. In the following section, I examine what it means to offer such a juxtaposition and analyze some of its inherent moral fallacies.

Israel and Multicultural Reverie

Much of the moral dubiousness I identify can be located in Taglit-Birthright, merely on the basis of its painful suggestiveness and apart from its problems as an actual travel-abroad program. The very notion of a birthright—of the right to make a political claim based solely or primarily on a biological identification—is profoundly unjust and has repeatedly caused bloodshed throughout history, especially during the era of European colonization. The continued usage of birthright as a historical claim is currently causing bloodshed in Palestine, a devastating variety resulting from settler colonization, in which Hillel directly implicates itself by promoting this base form of biological determinism. The idea of exclusive access based on biology or ethnic identification belies every meaningful form of civic responsibility.

At this point the conflation of civic responsibility with support for Israel becomes most damning. By promoting Taglit-Birthright as central to its mission, Hillel becomes in essence an ethnonationalist organization. There is no reason why Hillel should not thus be banned from participating in any form of multicultural celebration. It patently rejects any form of multicultural participation in its main policy issue. Yet according to a certain logic there is no contradiction between Hillel's ethnonationalism and its supposed commitment to multicultural participation as exemplified by its 2008 summit. That logic pervades discourses of American multiculturalism in general, suggesting that customary shows of support for Israel enhance multicultural community. In many multicultural communities, this support has become perfunctory (in Virginia Tech's, for example). Israel and Jewishness so ardently become coterminous that agents of multicultural celebration come to believe that excluding Israel from activities is the same as excluding Jews. This belief usually comes into existence through the inverse: Jewish Zionists use the coterminous relationship of Israel and Jewishness to interject promotion of Israel into multicultural celebration.

What are the ethical consequences of the coterminous relationship of Israel and Jewishness? They are many, none of them positive. First of all, it means that Israel cannot be included in multicultural celebrations without reflecting negatively on Jewish people, many of whom do not want to be identified in any way with the nation-state or who do not want the nation-state to be their primary cultural identity. Second, it entraps Jewish people in an unsavory paradigm, one in which they perform gruesome acts because of their culture. If Israel is the embodiment of Jewish culture, then it is being entrusted with a sort of authority that no nation-state can execute favorably. Herein lies the main problem of conjoining culture and national character. Hillel and other Jewish civic organizations render themselves distinctly responsible for Israel's violence by proclaiming themselves guardians of the state's consciousness. Moreover, they perform a nonconsensual appropriation of all Jewish people into the service of state policies that render the culture indefensible along with the state policies that are said to arise from the culture. It is never a good idea, even through the trope of strategic essentialism, to link an ethnic group to a military apparatus. Such a move automatically justifies discourses—in this case anti-Semitic ones—that should never be justifiable.

These issues exist within the broader problem of cultural identity as it is located in the construct of the nation-state. As Iris Marion Young explains, "States are public authorities that regulate the activities of those within their jurisdictions through legal and administrative institutions backed by the power to sanction."[7]

Young rejects the model of sovereignty through the nation-state model, arguing that the "legitimate claims of indigenous peoples today for self-determination cannot be fully met within the existing system of global governance that assumes the nation-state as the primary political actor."[8] When Israel was created in 1948—as, to a lesser degree, now—the model of liberation through acquisition and control of a state predominated. The idea that Jews could control their own destiny led to a movement in which Jewish control over a sovereign landmass would presumably solve the problems of anti-Semitism and perpetual minority status. Now that Israel has been a nation-state for over sixty years, it is easy to observe that the original goals of Zionism were a failure. Jews do not appear to be any safer now than they ever were. Anti-Semitism has not been cured. Jews are no more liberated than any other ethnic group whose cultural identity has been articulated through the nation-state.

I also deem Zionism a failure because it not only requires the ethnic cleansing of Palestinians but also is based on an inherently unjust model of liberation. Even if Israel as a nation-state had no Palestinians to exclude from normative citizenship, it would have Jews and other ethnic minorities to marginalize, for no nation-state's identity encompasses the cultural diversity of its population. Like all movements seeking liberation through a state apparatus, Zionism is imbued with national mythologies. One, Nur Masalha explains, has been especially prevalent: "It is important politically for the Zionists to predicate a constant and enduring Jewish presence in Palestine, and in the city of Jerusalem in particular. But the claim that political Zionism expressed 2,000 years of yearning for Jewish political and religious self-determination is a modern myth—invented in Europe in the mid to late nineteenth century."[9] The desire of Zionism to produce a sovereign nation-state solely for Jews is one that cannot have existed before the European Enlightenment; it was in the aftermath of the Enlightenment that the notions of liberation central to Zionism were developed, in addition to the racial taxonomies from which Jewish ethnonationalism arises.

Even assessing the philosophical and political origins of Zionism is unnecessary if our goal is to illustrate the problematic dimensions of its ethnocentrism. It does not simply represent a movement to liberate Jews from anti-Semitism, or a constellation of national mythologies, or the construction of a nation-state. Zionism remains an ethnonationalist movement, a fact that too often is ignored or forgotten by scholars and activists who accommodate it in humanist spaces as if it were merely an innocent appendage of Judaism or Jewish culture. The claims by organizations like Hillel that Israel is a physical manifestation of Jewishness tacitly reduce cultural identity to ethnocentric affiliation, creating a highly politicized version of culture, one that is historically shortsighted. These are the ethical and philosophical problems with Zionism, as indeed with all forms of national identity that rely on strict versions of cultural belonging in order to engender community.

Zionism's political problems are more conspicuous. In *The Abolition of White Democracy*, Joel Olson points out a central flaw of racialized belonging in the United States:

> Citizenship is a political identity signifying equality in the public sphere and the shared enjoyment of rights and duties, including the all-important right to participate in governing public affairs. American citizenship, however, historically has also been a form of social status that has served to distinguish those who were or could become full members of the American republic from those who could not.[10]

Olson examines how notions of race have influenced American jurisprudence and its conceptions of democratic citizenship. These notions have been performed with much complexity throughout American history, but there has been a consistent equation of whiteness with both legal and conceptual Americanness. But the United States has largely evolved beyond the era of racially inscribed citizenship in a legislative framework; the valuation of citizenship based on race, appearance, religion, and so forth now happens as a de facto phenomenon. Many legislative initiatives after 9/11 complicate what it means to belong to the American national polity, especially for Arabs and Muslims caught within the many ambiguous areas of unconstitutional prosecution. Nevertheless, the United States adheres to a legal definition of citizenship that does not, or is not supposed to, take into account religion, culture, race, gender, and so forth.

Israel has no ability to overcome the types of juridical problems inherent in the United States, however. Israel is not an open or even a participatory democracy. It is a state whose definition of national belonging is limited to those of a particular ethnic group. More crucial, unlike every other nation-state, Israel supposedly represents a demographic that is not consistent with its actual population. It is not merely beholden to its 7 million citizens, a substantial portion of whom it mistreats (the non-Jewish Palestinians); it is also the central state of Jews worldwide, no matter what their technical nationality. Israel's 1.5 million Palestinian citizens are decidedly less a part of Israel's national identity than the Jewish American college kids who do Taglit-Birthright as an exotic break from their suburban lives of McMansions and shopping malls. Although many non-Israeli Jews reject the onus with which Zionists have endowed Israel, it is indubitably a part of Israel's national character to act as synecdoche of Jewishness. As to the Taglit-Birthright vacationer-crusaders, there is something more than mere ethnic affiliation that makes their visits to Israel appropriate. Israel presents simply another form of ethnic segregation with which they are familiar in their privileged lives in the United States.

Israel's biggest obstacle to achieving the sort of democratic humanism of which it boasts is the composition of the state itself. Israel at its most basic is thus an ironic fantasy: in order to actualize its ideals, it would cease to exist as it is presently constituted. Its foundational legislation, along with hundreds of other legal infelicities, limits Israel to its colonial origin. The Law of Return is the most egregious marker of Israel's ethnonationalism. The law limits immigration to Israel solely to Jews (an amorphous category, like all religious or ethnic identifications). A white American of French or English background who converts to Judaism can immediately attain inherent rights of citizenship that no Palestinian—not even the citizens of Israel—can access. It is from this exclusivist notion of belonging that programs such as Taglit-Birthright develop their allure to those who feel chosen to do something special in reinforcing Jewish nationhood. That they outfit this deadly serious reclamation mission with happy-go-lucky narratives of fun and adventure does not signal depravity as much as it does shrewd marketing of political ideology as natural reality.

Yet it is not merely through its strident ethnonationalism that Zionism fails to achieve the sort of enlightened modernity it fervently broadcasts. Zionism underlines a state engaged in overt and covert violence of ferocious dimensions. Israel's violence has existed well beyond its own borders, affecting places like Central America, South Africa, and the United States (most notably through the 1967 attack on the USS *Liberty*, which killed thirty-four U.S. servicemen and was promptly exculpated by the American Congress).[11] Israel has put Zionists, both ardent and progressive, on the wrong side of nearly every issue of global import. I identify a range of adherents of Zionism in the previous sentence to highlight my contention that any sort of favorable identification with Zionism embroils one in Israel's belligerence even if one consciously opposes the injustices around the world in which Israel is complicit or directly involved. A soft Zionist—defined here as somebody who identifies as liberal but abandons that liberalism vis-à-vis Israel—during the 1970s who adamantly opposed South African apartheid was nevertheless complicit in it through his or her support of Israel, even if that support was tepid or conditional on withdrawal from the Occupied Territories. This is so because any legitimizing factor of Israel contributes to its aspirations of normative permanence. These aspirations are in dialectic with innate state violence, however. Anybody who identifies favorably with Zionism at least tacitly supports juridical racism, legal segregation, military occupation, ethnic cleansing, and land appropriation, in addition to the more specific policies of removing Arabic from road signs, restricting Arab residence in Jewish neighborhoods, and predicating citizenship on oaths of loyalty to Israel as a Jewish-majority state. My judgment about all Zionists' complicity in these horrors may seem harsh, but I am thinking carefully about the implications of casual engagement with an ideology whose agents are known to effect brutality. It is viable to surmise that one is responsible for even the most flippant of beliefs, and certainly for passionate ones. To claim Zionism as an outlook or identity, even tenuously, is to take ownership of the violence it generates.

These issues rarely enter into conversations about the presence of Jewish culture celebrations on campus and elsewhere. The main reason for their absence is the success of event organizers in conceptualizing Israel as a national manifestation of Jewish culture, worthy of celebrating on the same level that commemorations of ethnic landmarks occur. Multicultural offices or their equivalents on campus are sensitive both to charges of anti-Semitism and cultural insensitivity if they limit the participation of Israel (something many of them would be disinclined to do, anyway, based on their political sympathy with or adherence to Zionism). The normatization of Israel in American discourses of multiculturalism is so absolute that it is nearly impossible to criticize Israel without the concomitant burden of disrespecting Jews. Of particular interest is that Palestinians never play into this dynamic because they have so thoroughly been disassociated from the Holy Land. University administrators can therefore exclude and obstruct Palestinians from multicultural participation. In fact, the inclusion of Palestinians ipso facto often provokes anger and charges of insensitivity. The inverse of this situation is that when Israel misbehaves, all Jews, no matter where, become responsible. This burden is untenable and inappropriate but inevitable if the conception of Israel as pervasively representative of world Jewry is going to be so ardently enforced.

The frequent inclusion of Zionism in multicultural spaces, both physical and metaphorical, enables us to think more closely about the utility of multiculturalism as a discourse and a practice. Zionism represents centers of power financially and politically. It is an ideology (or set of ideologies) deeply inscribed in state power all over the world. It supports an enormous military economy and an imperialism whose reach is capacious. It partakes of the capitalist structures of neoliberalism that expropriate resources from the Southern Hemisphere into the Northern. Zionism is inseparable from the forces of structural injustice that occur throughout the world. My point here is not to suggest that Zionism corrupts multiculturalism, though that is likely the case, at least in the abstract. I suggest instead the possibility that multiculturalism itself is problematic because it so easily accommodates Zionism (and other troublesome ideologies). Is the point of multicultural consciousness to oppose unjust power and racism? Or is it to provide spaces within institutions where ethnic minorities can escape racism? What is the point of using multicultural apparatuses to promote Israel as the apogee of Jewishness?

These questions are interrelated. The forms of multiculturalism familiar to most Americans are derived from employee or student pressure, public relations, and in some cases legal mandate. Most formal multicultural spaces, then, are reliant on the same institutions whose economic and political cultures necessitated these spaces in the first place. Although I have rarely heard it stated that multiculturalism is supposed to oppose power, it frequently appeases it, a judgment I base on nothing more than its continued existence. Academic and corporate institutions are set up to regulate and efficiently eliminate both internal and external challenges to their modes of governance and authority. In many ways, the promotion of multiculturalism is a diversion or a delusion, or perhaps simply a safe outlet for anybody who is marginalized to direct energy at symptoms rather than structures of problems. The evidence for this assessment is the deep-seated racism that still exists in the institutions wherein the idea of multiculturalism was invented.

It may be optimistic to imagine that multiculturalism can or was intended to be an antidote or challenge to racism. Virginia Tech's office of Multicultural Programs and Services "exists to assist Virginia Tech in creating a welcoming environment that affirms and celebrates the diversity of its community particularly those from underrepresented and historically marginalized populations." "MPS," the statement continues, "provides opportunities for dialogue across differences, student leadership training, cultural celebrations, mentoring, organization advising, faculty interaction, diversity training and community building."[12] At nearby Radford University, Multicultural and International Student Services is said to develop "cultural awareness, understanding and a sense of belonging among Radford University students on our campus and in our community."[13] At Yale University, the Intercultural Affairs Council reportedly "strives to support an inclusive and diverse campus environment that: engages in community dialogue; promotes cultural awareness, respect and appreciation; and challenges bias on the basis of race and ethnicity, gender, religion, sexual orientation, disability, social class, or other distinction."[14] In the Multicultural Student Center at the University of Wisconsin–Madison, the goals are similar: "The UW-Madison campus values diversity and the MSC has been providing opportunities by which differences can be celebrated."[15] I have scanned the websites of multicultural offices at over a hundred universities ranging from research extensive to liberal arts to four-year colleges to regional comprehensives, and all of their mission statements are similar, almost uniformly focused on climate, awareness, and dialogue.

The situation is the same in the corporate world, where multiculturalism is usually replaced with the language of diversity. "At Microsoft," a statement by the software giant proclaims, "we define diversity broadly, beyond race, national origin, gender, age, disability, sexual orientation, or gender identity or expression."[16] The Coca-Cola Company is rather more whimsical: "Two assets give us the opportunity to keep this promise—our people and our brand. The Coca-Cola Company leverages a worldwide team that is rich in diverse people, talent and ideas. As a global business, our ability to understand, embrace and operate in a multicultural world—both in the marketplace and in the workplace—is critical to our sustainability."[17] Even Fox News Corporation, the scourge of decent liberals everywhere and exemplar of all that is evil in the world, states, "Our future rests in our collective ability to embrace change and leverage diversity through our leadership, productions, employment, procurement and continued community support. We believe that diversity is critical to our business strategy, and will improve our competitiveness and prospects for long-term success."[18]

A few aspects of these statements stand out. Neither the corporations nor the universities seem particularly concerned with injustice, a word, including its cognates, rarely found in multicultural discourses (types of discourses that include the term "diversity"). The words "advocacy" and "racism" are also absent, an omission that emphasizes a reliance on recondite kindness rather than on proactive involvement to effect improved work or study environments. The corporations' embrace of diversity illuminates the origin of multicultural consciousness in the United States. While the phenomenon has a grassroots element in its past, it is largely a response by various institutions to social pressure, something of an appropriation of real activist energy. Multiculturalism has never fundamentally challenged the institutions from which racism emerges; it was folded into these institutions and altered to complement their structures. Corporations value diversity, not for the sake of probity or social transformation (which would threaten the stability of their markets), but for its value in accreting profit. Diversity is an economic asset and a form of social capital more than it is a transformative initiative. In the corporate world, it is a mode of profit, a response to market conditions that demand adherence to multicultural principles; without the demand, the commitment would cease to exist. While this may be obvious, there is an important lesson in it, that resistance is promptly appropriated into unjust systems if it adheres to capitalist logic. The idea of multiculturalism has long focused on inclusivity in the extant marketplace rather than on any sort of systemic change wherein the racism, sexism, and homophobia produced by the marketplace can be threatened. The dialectic between capitalist economies and deep-seated racism is so entrenched that it would be impossible to fulfill the promise of multiculturalism without abrogating the same institutions that created it.

The position of diversity in universities isn't very different, though the language surrounding it is less explicitly capitalistic. Universities generally adhere to a more organic notion of belonging and participation, but it is worth remembering that universities rarely discuss profit in any capacity, though it is a ubiquitous consideration. The mission statements of multicultural offices (or their equivalents) illustrate a commitment to the reputation of host institutions, not to any palpable form of justice or equality. If one wants to argue that these considerations should not be the domain of the multicultural office, then I will not disagree; I will instead suggest that the activist connotations that accompany multiculturalism therefore be problematized. Activism was never written into the agenda of multiculturalism, which has a corporate origin and exists mainly in the realm of public relations. While it is worth thinking about justice and equality in the framework of multiculturalism, it is important to contemplate the relationship of formal sites of multicultural recognition with the inherent forms of iniquity that underline the need for inclusiveness and understanding. Multiculturalism is too encumbered in state apparatuses to become an effective site of resistance, though it can provide a useful framework for dialogue and analysis.

Zionism's fluid participation in multiculturalism is enough to expose some of its basic problems. Israel can be accommodated in multicultural spaces because these spaces are often constituted by the same institutional apparatuses that nourish the state power Israel represents. In fact, Israel uses the discourses around inclusiveness, tolerance, and liberal participation that are central to celebrations of multiculturalism. Just as the structures of American racism are invariably unchallenged in institutional sites of multiculturalism, the juridical segregation endemic to Israel is actively ignored any time the nation is called up to embody Jewish culture. Even though there is a profound correlation between the mythologies of Zionism and multiculturalism, it does not mean that the correlation should go unchallenged.

Abolishing Ethnic Cleansing

We need to kick Israel out of multiculturalism. There are many reasons I make this argument despite my skepticism about the utility of multiculturalism as a model of meaningful contestation:

- Although multiculturalism has a corporate origin and often performs in accordance with corporate interests, it is nevertheless supposed to offer a productive site of dialogue for students and employees of color. Having symbols of Zionism displayed in such sites can be disconcerting to Arabs and Muslims, along with the many people of color opposed to Zionism.
- The inclusion of Zionism in multiculturalism contravenes basic multicultural principles of antiracism and community, for Zionism is predicated on racialist notions of belonging.
- By attempting to be inclusive of anybody with a claim to diversity, multiculturalism deemphasizes the needs of people of color by equalizing all forms of difference, regardless of societal power dynamics. Zionism contributes to this marginalization of minority discourses by occupying spaces it doesn't need in order to be heard. Israel is more a part of the American mainstream than most phenomena native to the United States.
- Zionism conceptualizes Israel as the embodiment of Jewish culture, an appropriation that is inaccurate and, arguably, culturally insensitive. It therefore excludes from multicultural participation Jews who oppose Zionism or do not identify with Israel.

The final point is of special import. Zionism represents an immoral form of ethnonationalism. It does not belong in any discourse that purports to be inclusive or humanistic. Jewish people have a right to be represented in multicultural celebrations and, like all other ethnic communities, have a right to share their cultural traditions with others. They should not have the right, however, to exalt a nation-state engaged in various modes of ethnic cleansing under the guise of innocent cultural exposition. If Jews want to participate in multiculturalism, we should ask them to leave Israel behind.

Zionism not only essentializes and misrepresents Jewish cultures; it also infringes on the right of Arab Americans to represent their viewpoints and traditions. It does so connaturally; that is to say, Zionism cannot exist beyond a bullying and chauvinistic posture. Its primary model of engagement is inevitably confrontational. There are very few examples of Zionism being used in the service of civic discourse vis-à-vis Palestinians. It is innately hostile to any sort of colloquy or coexistence with Arabs (and all other non-Jews). But how does it infringe on the right of Arab Americans to represent their viewpoints and traditions? Surprisingly, it does so in numerous ways. A pretty generic memory I have summarizes them nicely.

When I was at the University of Wisconsin–Whitewater a few years ago, the chair of my department helped organize a campus-wide forum on various issues relevant to the liberal left. He asked me if I would speak about Israel's occupation. I consented. The day before the forum, the schedule was released. There was a speaker on health care, one on Iraq, one on gay marriage, one on civil liberties, one on feminism, one on pacifism, and so forth. But there were two on Palestine: in addition to me there was a Zionist well known on campus for agitating on behalf of Israel and lodging complaints of anti-Semitism as his primary mode of communication. Our panels were simultaneous. I went on with the presentation, though I was displeased by the arrangement. My displeasure was not because of an outsize ego but because of an acute sense of malfeasance developed after years of similar experiences. It appears to be an unwritten dictum on the liberal left that criticism of Israel can never occur without the simultaneous presence of a supporter of Israel. No other issue required two speakers. It is not an accident that Palestine did.

If I were more sensitive, I would have taken the invitation of another speaker on Palestine to mean that my chair didn't trust in my knowledge or thought I would be too biased (perhaps the stupidest reason people use to oppose commentators). I also considered the possibility that he expected such a big audience that it would take two sessions to accommodate it. That theory imploded when I entered a two-hundred-seat auditorium. The fact is, my chair believed in my abilities completely and had no logistical dilemma to sort out. Not even his opinion on the Israel-Palestine conflict was of particular influence in his scheduling. He was merely following the rules of liberal multiculturalism: all issues can be presented with a tendentious viewpoint, including the Israel-Palestine conflict, as long as it is discussed by a Zionist; any Arab presenter must be counteracted by a Zionist not for the sake of thoroughness but in the interest of the abruptly sacred trope of "balance." Zionists have convinced devoted multiculturalists that their ideology is a hallowed element of liberal discourse and that to exclude it is tantamount to tacit anti-Semitism. In this way, Zionism controls the terms of debate without conspicuous intimidation.

The assumptions inherent in this scenario are ugly and often racist. They are tied to a sort of power wherein the colonizer, in this case Israel, determines the political and philosophical destiny of its subjects. There is also an element of fear here, an unwillingness to let Israel be discussed without the oversight of its custodians, lest a pesky anti-Zionist become unacceptably critical (defined as challenging the sacrosanct belief that Israel has an innate right to an eternal Jewish majority). This situation is a form of discursive colonization. Palestinians and other Arabs cannot access the resources of the multicultural office without Zionist supervision, but they are powerless to challenge the preponderance of Zionism in the multicultural office. Aside from the institutional auspices of universities and corporations, Palestinians and other Arabs are made to justify the very existence of their cultural and political narratives. To oppose Zionism in the United States is to immediately enter into the abstract but consequential realm of irresponsible, radical, terroristic, extreme, or whatever other term can be used as an automatic invalidation. The devoted multiculturalist can be none of these.

I recount this rather immaterial memory because it is one example of how a multicultural commitment to Zionism can help marginalize Arabs and Muslims. The notion of proportional representation that Zionists invoke whenever they are not in control of dialogue around the Israel-Palestine conflict is never actually proportionate; it is a demand to anti-Zionists to cede their right of unfettered expression. There is no real marketplace of ideas when it comes to the Israel-Palestine conflict; there is instead a contest whose parameters rarely exclude Zionist participation. The moment that an anti-Zionist voice is burdened with its counterpart in the service of balance, all semblance of intellectual integrity has been compromised. The problem with balance is that it's never truly balanced; even if we could achieve true balance, it would be undesirable. Nobody should seek balance as a form of intellectual engagement; truth is a much better goal. Balance is merely a sneaky way to maintain extant power structures.

Balance isn't just passively conciliatory; it is actively destructive. It achieves this destructiveness by delegitimizing the viewpoints its champions find unsavory regardless of their basis in law or scholarly research. Balance is never invoked as a desirable feature of debate unless a specific group or position is being undermined. Multicultural discourse is especially vulnerable to this type of pressure. It is concerned with equal representation and inclusiveness, two ideas that sound good in the abstract but that are routinely manipulated for the sake of ideologies that contravene multicultural principles. Zionism thoroughly illuminates the problem of undiscriminating modes of multicultural celebration.

Creating Exclusive Inclusiveness

No ideology more than Zionism has the ability to make hypocrites of even the sincerest human beings. People who adamantly oppose all forms of segregation, militarism, torture, and colonization nevertheless support Israel despite each of these actions being a hallmark of the state. How is this support possible?

There is no easy answer to this question, but we can uncover some useful observations through careful analysis, something I aim to accomplish throughout this book. Israel markets itself as a lonely democracy surrounded by barbarism, something all good liberals amorous of modernity would naturally support. More entrenched is that Zionists have so adamantly conflated all Jews with Israel that the state assumes a unique status as a cultural paragon. This conflation is clear in the many expositions of Jewish culture in which

Israel becomes paramount both to Jews and Judaism. The representations of Israel are always specific to food (appropriated from pan-Syrian cuisine), land (from the river to the sea), identity (a space promised to all Jews), and the arts (a normative, timeless Western place). The representations, in other words, pretend to be apolitical while performing deeply sectarian work under the guise of innocent cultural interchange. Perhaps the most sectarian politicking happens through a uniform omission: the Palestinians are never anywhere to be found in these cultural celebrations except implicitly in the elements of their culture that Zionists have invented and then presented as their own.

When a multicultural office displays the paraphernalia of Zionism, it might imagine itself to be doing the good work of promoting Jewish culture. In reality, however, it is endorsing Zionist ethnonationalism. All sorts of mythologies contribute to the idea of Israel as an apolitical manifestation of timeless Jewish culture, something I explore in the chapters that follow. The primary mythology of concern here is the one suggesting that, as in the Holy Land, Zionists have an exclusive right to participation in narratives from which the Palestinians are completely absent. Unlike most ethnic disputes, this one is a zero-sum game: there is no way for Zionism and Palestinians to coexist. The basic terms of Zionism disallow any satisfactory form of Palestinian self-determination or self-representation. In choosing to include Zionism, then, multicultural offices are at least tacitly opting to exclude Palestinians and other advocates of real democracy. This is how I felt when I entered the multicultural office at Virginia Tech. It became a place in which I and other Arabs were markedly unwelcome, a place where the specter of ethnonationalism betrayed the promise of safety and belonging.

The incompatibility of Zionism with any type of antiracist consciousness was exposed by trickster videographer Max Blumenthal and his colleague Joseph Dana in 2009. Blumenthal traveled to Jerusalem and interviewed numerous Taglit-Birthright college students about President Barack Obama's Cairo address to the Muslim world. Their reactions, from a bar scene that resembled Madison, Wisconsin, much more than the Middle East, are eye-opening. One man calls Obama a "fuckhead" and a "shithead," following with "White power! Fuck the niggers!" "Oh, he's a Muslim for sure. . . . He's not from the U.S.; he's like a terrorist," a woman opines. Another man jokes that he wants "to eat watermelon with Obama" and then makes an incomprehensible remark about "niggers." A different interviewee seems incapable of saying anything other than "Fuck Obama."[19] Blumenthal and Dana were criticized for interviewing supposedly drunk college students and exploiting them for sensationalistic quotes. Yet Blumenthal produced a video shortly thereafter in which he interviewed completely sober people expressing identical sentiments. The opinions the American college students express in the original video are in no way an aberration; they represent the logical outcome of Zionist morality.

Because Blumenthal is Jewish, the students felt an affiliation that they imagined would protect them from the reproach of outsiders. In other words, it was in a hermetic Zionist context that they raised their comments; as a result, the comments were much sincerer than those that the students would have provided to, say, CNN. The students' comments also reflect systemic racism in Israel. An Association for Civil Rights in Israel (ACRI) poll conducted in December 2007 "reve[a]led that Israeli youths are bombarded with stereotypic, racist imagery, and their opinions have developed accordingly: Over two-thirds [of] Israeli teen[s] believe Arabs to be less intelligent, uncultured and violent."[20] An ACRI poll from March 2007 showed that 50 percent of Israelis "said they would not live in the same building as Arabs, will not befriend, or let their children befriend Arabs and would not let Arabs into their homes."[21] The December poll revealed that 81 percent of Israelis want Jewish National Fund land, 13 percent of Israel's territory, to be reserved for the exclusive use of Jews. This state land, it should be pointed out, was stolen from Arabs.

As Blumenthal's subjects indicate, Zionist racism is not limited to Arabs. On January 8, 2008, the Israeli daily *Ma'ariv* printed a cartoon showing Obama painting the White House black.

The cartoon indicates that Obama is spoiling a pristine tradition of whiteness with a sort of black immutability that will forever alter American demography and its decorous attitudes. The black is also a symbol of mourning, alluding to the mistaken belief among many Zionists that Obama is hostile to Israel. The cartoon suggests that Obama's ethnicity determines his outlook. Obama's election brought out other forms of Israeli racism. In 2009 Shas Party spiritual leader Rabbi Ovadia Yosef referred to Obama as a slave: "American insidiousness tells us to build here and not to build there as though we were slaves working for them. . . . We live in a time when slaves are governing us and are trying to control us."[22] Yosef's comment is reminiscent of the one offered a month earlier by Israeli Science and Technology minister Daniel Hershkowitz, who deemed Obama "Pharoah" in reference to the (presumably black) Egyptian enslaver of the ancient Jews.[23]

This racism is not isolated. Despite the fact that most Ethiopian Jews are devoted Zionists, in Israel they face institutional racism. A 2002 report published in the *Israel Equality Monitor* shows that Ethiopian Jews in Israel lag well behind white Jews in every relevant economic and social category. Forty-seven percent of Ethiopians are absent from the Israeli labor force, compared with 24 percent of Israel's total population; Ethiopian women were especially underrepresented. Levels of education and access to university study are deplorable. Opportunities for upward mobility are dramatically limited.[24] All of this is in addition to the constant skepticism by white Jews that the Ethiopians aren't adequately Jewish. Even when their claims to Jewish ceremonial practice are accepted, their biological claim to proper Jewishness is often rejected. Zionists take tribalism to depraved levels of chauvinistic exclusion, which is ironic given their insistence that they epitomize modernity.

The racism against black people in Israel, the vitriol against Obama, and the abominable attitudes toward Arabs are all interrelated. In fact, they arise from the same central ideology from which Zionism emerged as an ethnonationalist movement, one it continues to nurture today. It is the ideology of racialist access to citizenship and biologically determined ethics of communal belonging. What leads young white Americans to claim for themselves a land across the world that to them is little more than a mythologized entitlement is the same force that leads them to apply age-old epithets to Obama: it is a severe apathy toward the wellness of humanity, an inability to empathize with others, a sectarianism feeding and fed by dogmatic notions of inalterable difference based on superficial characteristics. It is, in short, the unavoidable outcome of Zionism. The youngsters on Blumenthal and Dana's video so eager to denigrate African Americans and Palestinians in the company of their ideological compatriots are the same ones who plaster symbols of their racism in multicultural centers and pass off these symbols as exemplars of Jewish humanity.

I know many readers will feel I should have said something to my friend, the multicultural director at Virginia Tech, if only to inform him of the loaded connotations of the Israeli flags of which he was probably unaware. I will not argue against this position. I imagine that an unacknowledged timidity or deference may have prevented me from speaking up. There was also the unshakable feeling that the multicultural office—this one, and all of them—is not the best site of struggle because ultimately it answers to the same power from which Zionism emerges. Expelling Zionism from civic institutions would be an important symbolic victory, however, and in that sense I have reversed my position of silence. There is a principle here that cannot be ignored, that of being excluded from a space I and other Arabs have a right to access. Wherever Zionism is exhibited we are explicitly unwelcome; its presence signifies the blight of colonization and arcane notions of nationhood. Administrators of multicultural apparatuses need to know of these significations because of their discomfiting implications. For those who disapprove of my silence, I hope you will accept my attempt at redemption: I intend to give my friend a copy of this book, along with a passel of Palestinian flags, because, unlike those to whom colonization and ethnic cleansing are unacceptable, multiculturalism is a place from which Zionists deserve expulsion.

2 Is the Anti-Defamation League a Hate Group?

> A lie with a purpose is one of the worst kind,
> and the most profitable.
>
> —FINLEY PETER DUNNE

The Anti-Defamation League (ADL) has a long and distinguished history. It was founded in 1913 by Chicago lawyer Sigmund Livingston to combat rampant anti-Semitism in the United States, which at the time entailed quotas on university admissions, the exclusion of Jews from various social and political communities, and even lynching. Nearly a hundred years later, Livingston might be surprised that his vision has grown into the powerful organization it is today. It is not only the ADL's level of potency that has evolved; its range of activity has expanded alongside its organizational growth. These two maturations are causal: it is the ADL's expanded range of activity that has engendered its substantial power. The ADL's success, however, has generated questionable commitments. After 1967 the ADL started to gradually emphasize sustenance of Israeli state policies in addition to battling anti-Semitism and thereby conflated the battle against anti-Semitism with ardent support for Israel. The ADL's support for Israel has not been conditional. It has been thoroughgoing. As a result, serious questions arise about the ADL's ethical, strategic, and political alliances. Audrey Shabbas asks, "Can an organization become a hate group toward some segments of the community, and still be accepted by the rest as a champion of human rights?"[1] This chapter endeavors to answer Shabbas's question using systematic analysis of the ADL's own definition of a hate group.

First, I assess the range of the ADL's political commitments in order to procure an accounting of its major activist emphases. Then I perform a discourse analysis of the ADL's explicit and tacit criteria for identifying a hate group. Finally, I measure the ADL's taxonomical formulas against its public advocacy to illustrate that according to its own discourses the ADL should be classified as a hate group. There are numerous reasons for this claim. I focus on three: (1) the ADL's resolute support of American imperialism and Israeli colonization, (2) the ADL's persecution of academics and public figures whose politics do not express adequate fealty to Israel, and (3) the ADL's institutional denial of genocide, in particular the 1915 Turkish genocide of Armenians. Any organization that concentrates on amorphous matters like race and representation will inevitably attract controversy. This naturally is true of the ADL, but I situate my analysis beyond discursive and definitional phenomena and instead explore the ADL's peculiar adherence to issues and viewpoints that would seem to belie its classification as a civil rights group. Very few civil rights groups, for instance, work so closely with the police apparatuses of the state. Indeed, the goal of many of these groups is to monitor and challenge those police apparatuses. In the case of the ADL, it works closely with the American state on various domestic and international practices, policing in particular, which orients it in a site of unusual authority. The ADL is therefore responsible morally for a range of state interventions that cast doubt on its ostensibly trenchant mission to monitor and eliminate anti-Semitism.

Before I enter into these analyses I provide some context. The ADL is an international organization, though the majority of its work takes place in the United States. It has thirty regional offices and three international offices, in Israel, Russia, and Italy. According to its 2008 annual report, the most recent available as of this writing, the ADL brought in over $66 million in public support and revenue, although its IRS Form 990, procured through a GuideStar search, also lists $2.06 million in noncash assets, for a total income of over $68 million.[2] The 2008 report claims an operating budget of nearly $69 million, broken into program and supporting services, resulting in a net asset decrease of $2.6 million. The ADL's total net assets, according to the report, decreased from $20.9 million at the end of 2006 to $18.3 million at the end of 2007.[3]

However, its IRS Form 990 lists only $64.5 million in spending in 2007, with $3.6 million noted as an unexplained change in its fund balances. In any case, according to its documents, the ADL emerges as an organization with an enormous operating budget and net assets in excess of $18 million. From 2003 to 2006, the ADL took in over $225 million in gifts, grants, and contributions.[4]

The ADL's most visible employee, Abraham Foxman, the national director who actively writes op-ed pieces and letters to the editor, earned over $266,000 in 2007, with over $55,000 contributed to his benefits and an expense account topping $16,000. Marshall Levin, the former director for national development, earned over $194,000, though it does not appear that he was actually employed by the ADL.[5] Deputy national director Kenneth Jacobson earned $201,600, with contributions to his benefits topping $74,000. The associate national director for regional operations, Ira Robert Wolfson, made nearly $190,000, with $63,000 in benefits. The director of education, Edgar Alster, pulled in over $176,000, and almost $50,000 in benefits.[6] What stands out about these salaries beyond their generous compensatory structure is that the ADL's leadership is highly concentrated among a few people and heavily male (the only salaried female employee listed in Form 990 is Los Angeles regional director Amanda Susskind, who was paid $185,800 in 2007). Although the organization lists hundreds of employees, the majority of its salary budget is devoted to a group of bureaucrats who exercise top-down power. The ADL also enlisted the services of Furman Roth Advertising, at $736,000; Convio Inc., a fundraising consultant firm, at $473,000; Sarkady Consulting, a leadership training service, at nearly $300,000; and OMP, a D.C.-based fundraising consultant, at nearly $200,000. At least twenty-nine contractors each received over $50,000 for services rendered to the ADL in 2007.[7]

I conducted this inquiry into the ADL in order to validate my claim that the organization is powerful. Its power can be discerned through not only its level of public visibility but also the amount of funds it is able to raise, the immensity of its operating budget, and the salaries it provides its leaders. The ADL enjoys a sort of financial prosperity far surpassing that of most civic or civil rights organizations. As a comparison, the Radius of Arab American Writers Inc. (RAWI), a nonprofit organization for which I served as executive director from 2005 to 2008, operates on an annual budget of less than $10,000; the ADL spends twenty-seven times that on printing services alone. This budget of the ADL does not bespeak anything other than fiduciary success. It tells us nothing about the ADL's mission or philosophy. It does not illuminate the tenor and effectiveness of its educational and political activities. And it cannot clarify the ways that the ADL's commitments might be usefully contextualized and interpreted. These are tasks I undertake in the following sections.

The ADL and Israel

For an organization supposedly devoted to the singular cause of eliminating anti-Semitism worldwide, the ADL spends a huge amount of time justifying any noteworthy Israeli political or military action. It likewise devotes plentiful resources to refuting, and sometimes aggressively delegitimizing, Israel's critics. The ADL's promotional materials emphasize the sanctity of Israel to Jewish culture and identity, a claim that would be difficult to dispute, one that in any case is virtually meaningless to my current analysis. One need not attempt to dispute the ADL's claim in order to impugn it. By conflating Israel with Jewishness and conceptualizing support of Israel as a Jewish duty, the ADL constructs an ethical paradigm in which criticism of Israel as a nation-state becomes open to assessment as culturally insensitive commentary. It also consigns itself to endorsement or dissemination of profoundly racist ideals.

The ADL's critics believe that the organization's primary goal is to protect Israel from any negative commentary, a goal that the ADL rationalizes by equating negative commentary about Israel to a tacit attack on Jewish people. In the *San Francisco Weekly*, Matt Isaacs points out that the ADL's "critics, whose political and religious affiliations vary widely, repeatedly describe the ADL as a self-appointed agent of Israel that cloaks itself in the rhetoric of fighting hate, while actively attempting to silence those who are not hatemongers, but mere opponents of Israeli government policy."[8] The ADL's literature doesn't belie these suspicions. The first two pages of its 2008 annual report focus on Israel, with headlines such as "Making the case for Israel's operation in Gaza" and "First to defend Jews against a furious backlash."[9] The report displays full-page newspaper advertisements sponsored by the ADL during Israel's December 2008–January 2009 invasion of the Gaza Strip, which human rights groups estimate killed over 1,400 Palestinian civilians, including over 300 children.[10] The ads are juxtaposed in a remarkably suggestive way, where "Jews to the Gas" leads into "Support Israel Now!" The report claims that "Israel's operation in Gaza ignited a firestorm of global anti-Semitism not seen in decades."[11]

A few things stand out about this rhetorical and visual strategy. First, as is common in ADL pamphlets and advertisements, the ADL proffers alarmist phrases such as "firestorm of global anti-Semitism" that are quantitatively indemonstrable and therefore coercive and hyperbolic. In fact, one of the ADL's own reports notes that anti-Semitic incidents in the United States declined for four straight years from 2005 to 2008,[12] and a Tel Aviv University report found that in 2008 anti-Semitic incidents worldwide decreased by 11 percent.[13] The report found a spike in anti-Semitism during January 2009, amid Israel's Gaza invasion, followed by a steep decline in February and March. However, much of what the report conceptualized as anti-Semitism was images in cartoons and demonstrations comparing Israel's behavior to that of Nazi Germany. While such comparisons are problematic historically, they are viable ethically in that attributions of brutal violence on the part of Israel, as with Nazi Germany, speak accurately to its widely documented human rights abuses. To deem such comparisons anti-Semitic creates an ethical framework in which inordinate violence can be justified as an act of justice. It is worth noting that numerous cases of anti-Semitic vandalism in 2007 and 2008 were found to actually have been committed by Jews.[14] In any case, it could be argued on the basis of patterns of documented anti-Semitic incidents that Israel does not provoke anti-Semitism, as the ADL and others suggest, but that Israel in fact generates anti-Semitism. It is likely that Israel's inhumane behavior, not mysterious repositories of predisposed hate, produce increases in what numerous groups deem anti-Semitic incidents (itself a process not without myriad problems). The ADL is culpable in this particular source of anti-Semitism because it is one of the most aggressive exponents of the idea that Israel and Jewishness are indivisible. That idea conjoins cultural practice with state action, a terribly perilous move socially and morally because it fosters an unsustainable ethnonational identity that transfers the burdens of violence from the state to the cultural group it supposedly embodies.

The ADL further conjoins total support of Israeli policies to responsible participation in American multiculturalism. Immediately following Barack Obama's well-received June 2009 address from Cairo to Muslims, the ADL expressed various intonations of displeasure. Attributing "the suffering of the Palestinian people" to "Arab wars," ADL national chair Glen S. Lewy and Foxman released a statement upbraiding Obama for his shortsightedness:

> Regarding the Israelis and Palestinians, it would have been important to hear the President put the conflict into its proper historical perspective—six Arab nations attacked Israel from day one and the occupation of Palestinian land was a product of Israel's wars of self-defense. While strongly reiterating the importance of America's relationship with the State of Israel and articulating Israel's right to exist, President Obama missed the opportunity to address the misperceptions in the Arab world and to make clear that the Palestinians would have had a state had they accepted the United Nations resolution in 1948 [sic].[15]

An op-ed by Foxman is even more explicitly critical. He lectures, "[Obama will] need now to find another occasion to make clear that Israel is legitimate because of the Jewish people's historic connection to the land, not because of Jewish suffering in Europe."[16] Foxman kept at it, later complaining in the *Jewish Week*, "And elements of concern—lack of context on the Arab-Israeli conflict, the failure to mention the historic Jewish connection to the land as the basis for Israel's legitimacy, the impression of equating the Holocaust with Palestinian suffering, the possible weakening of the U.S. position on Iran—have also been enumerated."[17]

Foxman's opinion of the Obama speech is debatable, but his historical claims are indemonstrable, having been exposed as mythologies by a plethora of scholars and journalists. The notion that Jews have a historical connection to Palestine beyond spiritual veneration is widely disputed; even if Foxman's version of history is correct, it does nothing to clarify the many problematic moral valuations that arise in asserting a cultural right to geographical space, primary among them the use of that invented right as a justification for colonization.[18] Moreover, the notion that Palestinians and Arab states have aggressively rejected peace whereas Israel has earnestly sought it has been thoroughly discredited by dozens of historians.[19] Only the uninformed or willfully ignorant now put forward such a view. In the face of documentary evidence that contravenes Zionist claims about the history of Jews in Palestine, in both the past and present, Foxman, like similar culture warriors, resorts to the invocation of a mythologized history in order to elucidate contemporary political conflicts. This form of argumentation is useless intellectually and dubious ethically because, rather than illuminating history, it actually invents it on the basis of how interests of power in the present require history to be conditioned and propagated. It was this necessity of historical mythology as safe puissance that Foxman applied to Obama.

If the ADL's castigation of Obama for not being pro-Israel enough seems odd for an organization that says it is devoted to ending anti-Semitism, it is because Obama's speech in Cairo had nothing to do with anti-Semitism. The ADL, in other words, appropriated Obama's speech for the purpose of keeping the topic in play when it had no legitimate reason for inclusion. The passion and displeasure with which the ADL responded illustrates the level of its devotion to Israeli nationalism, concealed by the contextual discourse of attacking anti-Semitism. It is a strategy that the ADL has cultivated ever since Foxman's assumption of its national directorship in 1987. After intense lobbying in 2004, for example, the ADL convinced the influential Ford Foundation, sponsor of numerous multicultural initiatives, to "no longer fund organizations that incite anti-Semitism or challenge Israel's legitimacy."[20] The juxtaposition of anti-Semitism with Israel's legitimacy is typical, indicative once again of an appropriation of anti-Semitism for a supposedly grander purpose. The ADL's press release celebrating the decision notes,

> Responding to recent revelations that Ford Foundation grantees were active in the anti-Semitic, anti-Israel campaign at the 2001 U.N. World Conference Against Racism in Durban, South Africa, [Ford Foundation president]

Ms. Berresford said that no future grants would go to organizations that support terrorism, bigotry or the delegitimization of Israel.[21]

It is impossible to state definitively at this point what effect this move has had on the overall funding patterns of American groups working on issues of race and culture, but no matter what its material consequences have been (and they have no option but to be negative), we can discern a more basic lesson from the ADL's pressure on Ford: in the service of its pet cause, Israeli nationalism, the ADL is willing to damage the efficacy of civil rights communities with whom it is supposed to share a mission and an affinity. In the name of open-mindedness it performed a quintessentially doctrinaire maneuver. Its primary discursive strategy was yet again to conflate anti-Semitism with anti-Israelism (whatever that is—the ADL never tells us beyond suggesting that anything contravening state policy is unacceptable); it went a step further in this case and appended terrorism and bigotry to the delegitimization of Israel (another phrase with a negative connotation that doesn't actually tell us anything of moral or philosophical import).

An analysis of the ADL's press releases illustrates that there is a direct correlation between the urgency of its activism, particularly the vocabulary it deploys, and Israel being subject to widespread criticism for some type of brutality. While the ADL might argue that this correlation definitively links Israel and anti-Semitism, in reality it elucidates a need for the ADL to invoke anti-Semitism as a strategy to protect Israel from even mild condemnation. In testimony to the House Foreign Affairs Committee, ADL deputy national director Kenneth Jacobson demanded, "The United States must make clear to Arab leaders that their silence in the face of anti-Semitism in their media makes them complicit in this perpetuation of incitement."[22] Jacobson's testimony included use of words such as "demonized," "terrorism," "scapegoated," and "violent action." An ADL press release during Israel's 2009 invasion of Gaza explains, "As Israel's operation against the Hamas terrorist infrastructure in Gaza continues, expressions of anti-Semitism and offensive Holocaust imagery have 'reached a fever pitch' in the Arab press."[23] The ADL wasted little time before posting a FAQ on its website devoted to the proposition that "Israel is not at war or in conflict with the people of Gaza or the Palestinian people. Israel's action was directed against the terrorist organization Hamas and its operational infrastructure."[24]

These efforts are notable in several ways. The ADL appears to have consciously adopted the word "incitement" as a way to deflect attention from Gaza's mounting civilian casualties and onto the discourses it interprets as threatening to Israel (a rather fidgety proposition given these discourses' lack of military capability). The word "incitement" is reinforced by equally hyperbolic diction: "fever pitch," "rampant," "the complete eradication of the state of Israel." Depending on one's perspective, it's either comical or deranged that the ADL is so eager to blame Arab and other widespread dislike of Israel on cartoons rather than on Israel's actual behavior, which includes garrison settlement, land appropriation, heavy property damage, crop destruction, a racialized legal system, and the documented murder of civilians. But the main ethical issue lies elsewhere, in the ADL's peculiar vernacular. Its use of humanistic language to absolve Israel of its violence corresponds with its civil rights identity, but despite its perpetuation of its civil rights myth the ADL ignores truths that to others are easily accessible. It notes in its Gaza FAQ:

> Civilian injuries and death are regrettable and tragic and throughout its operation, Israel took serious measures to avoid harming civilians. The targets chosen by the Israel Defense Forces were Hamas operational centers, most of which were deliberately located in densely populated areas. The targets included Hamas command centers, training camps, rocket manufacturing facilities, storage warehouses and tunnels used to smuggle arms. It cannot be forgotten that Hamas cynically and deliberately put ordinary Palestinians in harm's way by establishing its terrorist infrastructure—manufacturing, storage, training and strategic planning—within densely populated areas, in homes, schools, mosques and hospitals.[25]

Let's compare these claims against human rights reports and documented journalism. First of all, the ADL's argument that Hamas operational centers are located in densely populated centers is thoroughgoing cant. Nobody has actually located these elusive Hamas operational centers of Zionist legend, and not a single residential center in the Gaza Strip is not densely populated. The ADL's argument, then, is impossible to disprove but also impossible to verify; as is its custom, the ADL conveys ideological fervor through descriptive ambiguity. Second, Hamas is a democratically elected government, not a "terrorist organization," as the ADL repeatedly calls it. This distinction might appear unimportant, especially to those who believe that state actors can be terrorists, but in reality it attests to a much broader problem with the ADL's rhetoric: its unwillingness to grant Palestinians the courtesy of accurate representation. There are myriad spaces in which contestation is appropriate in the Israel-Palestine conflict, but a certain level of representational decency must first be available, a possibility the ADL's inaccurate rhetoric forestalls.

As to the ADL's insistence that Israel never targets civilians, observers and investigators in Gaza tell a much different story. The Palestinian Center for Human Rights (PCHR), located in Gaza City, reports,

> According to PCHR investigations, which include statements from eye-witnesses, IOF [Israeli occupation forces] have perpetrated crimes amounting to war crimes against medical personnel working in the Gaza Strip, in clear violation of the (1949) Fourth Geneva Convention, which affords special protection to medical personnel. Since the launch of their military offensive against the population of the Gaza Strip on 27 December 2008, IOF have killed seven Palestinian medical personnel, and wounded dozens of others, whilst they were attempting to evacuate and transfer the dead and injured. IOF have launched ground, sea and air attacks targeting medical personnel and medical facilities, including ambulances, and in addition have obstructed the access of medical personnel to the dead and injured.[26]

A PCHR weekly report in January 2009, opens with this grim news: "The outcome of the IOF offensive on the Gaza Strip: entire families have passed away; children and women constitute more than 43% of the total number of victims; entire features of many areas have disappeared; and the civilian infrastructure services have completely collapsed."[27]

The Israeli human rights organization B'Tselem turned up virtually identical findings. In one case, B'Tselem reports, Israeli "soldiers had shot a woman waving a white flag and several civilians who were fleeing a bombed house on army orders."[28] B'Tselem's initial report concludes, "Most of the buildings Israel targeted in the Gaza Strip usually served civilian purposes, such as offices, mosques, and private houses." The report also notes, "Examination of the Israeli military's conduct during the operation raises concerns as to the extent to which Israel complied with its obligations under international humanitarian law regarding distinction, proportionality, and direct fire at civilians."[29] The Al Mezan Center for Human Rights published a report in April 2009 that clarifies the oft-repeated mythology that Palestinians use civilians as human shields. The disturbing report, "The Use of Palestinian Civilians as Human Shields by the Israeli Occupation Forces," presents seven case studies. One of these case studies recounts how Israeli soldiers used a ten-year-old Palestinian child as a human shield; another case study describes how an elderly Palestinian man was forced to run in front of soldiers. Other case studies explain how Palestinian civilians, including children and the elderly, were beaten, robbed, and killed in the process of being taken hostage by Israeli soldiers.[30] The Al Mezan report accords with numerous instances of similar behavior documented by human rights workers and investigators. In fact, Israel's use of Palestinian civilians as human shields is by now an indisputable feature of its army's behavior.[31]

Journalists have uncovered some horrifying stories that disprove the ADL's rhetoric. The *Times* of London confirmed that, during Operation Cast Lead, Israel's attack on the UN Relief and Works Agency (UNRWA) site, housing hundreds of civilians, was deliberate and involved the debilitating chemical white phosphorous, illegal for use in civilian areas.[32] According to UN investigators, "Israel violated a range of human rights during its invasion of Gaza, including targeting civilians and using a child as a human shield."[33] The UN investigations correspond with the eyewitness testimony of Norwegian physician Mads Gilbert, who was in Gaza during Israel's onslaught. "I've seen one military person among the tens—I mean, hundreds—we have seen and treated. So, anybody who tries to claim this as sort of a clean war against another army are lying. This is an all out war against the civilian Palestinian population in Gaza and we can prove that with the numbers."[34] Gilbert's assertion was indeed proved over and again, in one noteworthy case by the National Lawyer's Guild, whose February 2009 delegation to Gaza concluded that Israel violated numerous international laws, including the following:

- the principle of distinction by engaging in the willful killing of a number of Palestinian civilians;
- the principle of proportionality by carrying out a number of attacks where the "collateral damage" that resulted was vastly disproportionate to the direct military advantage that could have been achieved by Israel;
- customary international law on the use of weapons by misusing certain weapons, including the use of indiscriminate weaponry in residential and other heavily-populated civilian areas;
- the obligation to provide medical care to the wounded by deliberately denying or delaying access to medical care to wounded people; and
- the prohibition on attacking medical facilities or personnel.[35]

These reports bring to mind Chris Hedges's chilling observation, made eight years before Operation Cast Lead:

Yesterday at this spot the Israelis shot eight young men, six of whom were under the age of eighteen. One was twelve. This afternoon they kill an eleven-year-old boy, Ali Murad, and seriously wound four more, three of whom are under eighteen. Children have been shot in other conflicts I have covered—death squads gunned them down in El Salvador and Guatemala, mothers with infants were lined up and massacred in Algeria, and Serb snipers put children in their sights and watched them crumple onto the pavement in Sarajevo—but I have never before watched soldiers entice children like mice into a trap and murder them for sport.[36]

One needn't rely on the reports of human rights workers, lawyers, and journalists to determine that Israeli soldiers deliberately targeted civilians during Operation Cast Lead. One can simply listen to the Israeli soldiers themselves. The *Times* of London quotes one offender: "'That's the beauty of Gaza. You see a man walking, he doesn't have to have a weapon, and you can shoot him,' one soldier told Danny Zamir, the head of the Rabin pre-military academy, who asked him why a company commander ordered an elderly woman to be shot."[37] It is interesting that the soldier rendered the hypothetical victim a man when the actual victim was an elderly woman, which indicates that his action wasn't mere bloodlust, but the result of his well-trained consciousness. His offhand description of Gaza as a place of "beauty" is doubly troublesome: he utilizes that adjective because Gaza is one of the few places on earth where a human can partake of unmonitored violence. This soldier has plenty of company. According to the Voice of America, "[Yehuda Shaul] is collecting testimony from soldiers who fought in Operation Cast Lead, Israel's 22-day assault on militants [*sic*] in the Gaza Strip. He describes what he is hearing from the soldiers as 'disturbing.' He says some of the soldiers say their units were not advised to spare civilians."[38]

Taken together, the reportage and testimony gathered in the six months following Operation Cast Lead illustrate something much more brutal and systematic than occasional lapses of responsibility or circumstantial tragedy. The IOF engaged in one of the twenty-first-century's most vicious campaigns against civilians, one that was preceded and followed by the devitalizing economic sanctions that rendered the Gaza Strip an overcrowded space with high poverty and inadequate resources to sustain either a humanitarian infrastructure or a civil society. The ADL's repeated claim that militants had pervaded homes and hospitals, in which they installed a terrorist infrastructure, is completely indemonstrable. It is also remarkably stupid, for to people who aren't insane these sites of human interaction are usually called communities. Because it has been proved by reporters and investigators of various national and religious backgrounds and of myriad political identities that the IOF engaged in illegal and epidemic violence, then we have no choice but to conclude that the ADL's avid justification of that violence constitutes an archetypal form of incitement.

The ADL and Terrorism

After 9/11, the ADL seized the opportunity to enter into the business of monitoring Arab and Muslim terrorism. One of its main initiatives has been to work with law enforcement agencies at both local and federal levels. ADL literature boasts of the organization's role in gathering intelligence by "monitoring individual extremists and extremist groups."[39] If the thought of private organizations gathering intelligence on their compatriots isn't a comforting proposition, then the prospect of the ADL doing it is terrifying. I have general apprehensions about the desire of civil rights groups to monitor individuals and to work with law enforcement agencies, primary among them a well-informed suspicion about the ability or desire of law enforcement agencies to act ethically and about the processes by which individuals and groups might be dubbed extremist or dangerous. American history shows time and again that such designations have been abused or exploited in order to repress diverse forms of dissent. The ADL provides us a wonderful example of how these suspicions contain ample substantiation.

Unsurprisingly, the ADL's conception of terrorism is affected by its devotion to Israel. The ADL still directs many of its resources at neo-Nazi and white supremacist groups but also places much emphasis on what it calls Arab and Muslim extremists. These dual emphases aren't necessarily contradictory, but they do, by design, conflate strong criticism of Israel with neo-Nazism.[40] I limit my analysis to the ADL's definitions and taxonomies of terrorism and its participation in state policing institutions. It is difficult to determine just how ensconced the ADL is in these institutions, but if we take its claims at face value, its participation is extensive: "In the aftermath of 9/11, we recognized that the threat is not only domestic, but global. We have significantly increased our monitoring of Al-Qaeda and other terrorist Web sites, opened lines of communication with international groups monitoring extremism in Europe and elsewhere, and incorporated information about international terrorism into our law enforcement trainings."[41]

Like "love" and "stupidity," "terrorism" is an opaque word; how a person chooses to define it, no matter any attempt at dispassion, illuminates his or her politics. The ADL's politics are easy to discern, however. The organization works hard to conceptualize

Israel as victim of a depoliticized and irrational Muslim extremism, one that is innately hostile to Judaism and therefore naturally targeted at an innocent Israel. The ADL proffers some pretty heady charges: "An increasing number of American Muslim extremists have been involved in terrorist plots and conspiracies in the U.S. in which Jews or Jewish institutions have been targeted or been considered for attack since 9/11."[42] The same article asserts that "the Muslim extremist threat has become as [sic] significant and growing domestic terror threat."[43] Are these assertions demonstrable, or are they hyperbolic?

According to the FBI's annual threat assessment to the Senate Select Committee on Intelligence, domestic terrorism is currently of minor concern: "We judge any homegrown extremists in the United States do not yet rise to the numerical level or exhibit the operational tempo or proficiency we have seen in Western Europe. A range of factors inside the United States may contribute to a lower incidence of homegrown cells developing."[44] The FBI's confidence is warranted. Since 9/11, three major terrorist attacks in the United States stand out: the envelopes of anthrax in 2001, the 2009 assassination of Dr. George Tiller, and the 2009 Holocaust Memorial Museum shooting. None of these events was carried out by Muslims. All of them were perpetrated by elements of the same right-wing Christian crowd that the ADL praises for its support of Israel. In 2008 and 2009, no terrorist attacks were perpetrated by Muslims in the United States. In fact, statistics show that (almost exclusively white) Christian fundamentalists opposed to abortion and homosexuality have committed more acts of terrorism in the United States than any other group. The FBI's accounting of terrorist incidents in the United States from early 2004 to the end of 2008 lists one act of terrorism committed by a perpetrator classified as "Islamic Extremist" (the perpetrator ran a vehicle into a group of students in Chapel Hill, North Carolina, injuring nine and killing none); it lists eight acts perpetrated by those classified as "Secular/Political/Anarchist."[45] It is hard to tell where the ADL is uncovering this harrowing epidemic of Muslim fanaticism, but it certainly isn't in the files of the FBI or the Department of Homeland Security.

But what of the Arab and Muslim terrorism that has been preempted? The ADL brags that it has played a major role in helping law enforcement agencies thwart terrorism. Either the ADL is exaggerating or it is unusually efficacious, for Arab and Muslim Americans have committed virtually no terrorism in the United States. In any case, it might not be wise for the ADL to tout its influence on the pursuit of terrorists given the preponderance of suspects who have been found innocent (Sami Al-Arian, Muhammad Salah, Mazen Al-Najjar, Abdelhaleem Ashqar, and Michel Shehadeh, all Palestinian) and the number of cases that were either coerced or invented by zealous officers: the Liberty City Seven, a group of homeless immigrants in Miami who were said to have been plotting the destruction of the Sears Tower, though it appears they were simply trying to con an eager FBI agent out of money;[46] the 2009 synagogue bombing plotted by ostensible Muslims who turned out to have been ensnared by a corrupt FBI officer;[47] the Lodi, California, trial of Hamid Hayat, who was sentenced to twenty-four years in a case riddled with misconduct.[48] The pursuit of terrorism is just as much a business as it is a matter of public safety. The ADL participates in this business by helping set rhetorical agendas that emphasize Israel's interests and conceptualize these interests as universal. The pursuit of terrorism is also a critical matter of public relations, an area in which the ADL excels. Ultimately, all evidence shows that the epidemic of Muslim American terrorists is an outright myth.

I indicated earlier that the definition of terrorism is indeterminate, with the varying definitions reflecting the speakers' politics more than any sort of connotative accuracy. (The same is eminently true of my definition.) On the basis of its notion of terrorism, the ADL's politics might best be described as adamantly Zionist. In its international terrorist symbols database, the ADL identifies twenty-seven symbols belonging to twenty groups, a markedly small number. It is not because of laziness that the number is so small, though; it is because the ADL puts forward a collection that is overwhelmingly Muslim, eighteen of the twenty groups, to be exact. Sixteen of the groups are Arab, ten Palestinian. That half of the groups listed in the ADL's international terrorist database are Palestinian illuminates a profound commitment to a basal version of Zionism. The ADL consolidates organizations with vastly divergent ideologies into an unvarying classification as terrorist; it groups a small collective of American Indians, the Little Shell Pembina Band, with the KKK and neo-Nazis. One of the groups in its database, Hamas, is a legitimate state actor, as I noted earlier. Another, Hezbollah, is also a powerful political party with a complex civic presence in Lebanon. Other groups, such as the Palestinian Liberation Front, Palestinian National and Islamic Forces, and the Islamic Palestine Block [*sic*], are so marginal as to be virtually nonexistent, while some, such as the Democratic Front for the Liberation of Palestine and the Popular Front for the Liberation of Palestine, have long ceased to be relevant players in the Middle East.

The non-Arab groups in the database are puzzling choices. They include Al Shabaab, a group opposed to Somalia's central government and the presence of Ethiopian troops; the Kurdistan Workers Party, a Marxist-Leninist group advocating Kurdish nationalism; and the Kahane Movement, a Jewish extremist organization based on the teachings of the late rabbi Meir Kahane, a Brooklyn-born ideologue who advocated the violent transfer of Palestinians from the Holy Land. The inclusion of a Jewish group in this database might be viewed as a sign of the ADL's objectivity, but such a view would be mistaken. Quite the opposite is true. The Kahane Movement is all but defunct in Israel; it still has a residual presence in the United States, only in New York City, but its best days are well behind it, and the ADL fails to categorize it as a domestic terrorist organization. There are plenty of active Jewish terrorist groups that the ADL could have identified, including the Yesha Council (successor of the notorious Gush Emunim), Terror Neged Terror (TNT; Terror Against Terror), Defending Shield (Egrof Magen), and Revenge of the Babies. Each of these groups has perpetrated violence against civilians within the past year; each is more active than many of the Arab outfits blacklisted by the ADL. This list doesn't even take into account the settler mobs that regularly converge on West Bank towns like Al-Khalil (Hebron) and murder civilians and desecrate property. Nor does it take into account the IOF, whose categorization as a terrorist organization would require a much broader discussion than what I am able to provide here. I will point out, however, that the IOF engages in proven acts of massive bloodshed that result in pervasive fear and rampant death of innocents. There is a good argument to be made that the IOF routinely performs terrorism.

The ADL is either sloppy or unconcerned that anybody will take five minutes to analyze its document. It explains that "most of the Islamic group symbols include a Koran," but only seven out of eighteen include anything even loosely resembling a Qur'an.[49] The explanation relies on absurd Orientalist formulations. "Depending on the symbol, the Muslim holy book denotes one or more of the following similar, though not identical, ideas: that its teachings are the reason for the group's existence; that group members are especially pious; that the group views its actions as a religious duty; that the entire world should follow Islam; that the Koran justifies killing and conquest."[50] This interpretation is faulty. For instance, Hamas, one of the groups with a Qur'an in its logo, has never made any public statement about the entire world following Islam; such an ambitious goal is far beyond its purview or concern. The Muslim Brotherhood, another group that displays the Qur'an, is mainly interested in overthrowing the dictatorial governments in the Arab World that Israel and the United States adamantly support. More disturbingly, the ADL offers no context for these groups' supposed terrorism beyond Islam itself. It is the pious of Islam who are drawn to specious violence, and it is always religion, not politics, in control of that violence. Elementary analysis reveals that the ADL international terrorist database is ideologically incoherent and politically tendentious. In all of its manifestations, it is thoroughly worthless.

Finally, it is worth pointing out another major problem with the ADL's inclusion of the Kahane Movement in its terrorist database: the Kahane Movement and the ADL actually share important ideological commitments, even if their strategic choices and organizational structures vary. Both organizations conceptualize Israel as central to and indivisible from Jewish identity; both believe that sustaining Israel is a Jew's most important obligation; both are inflexibly opposed to any sort of Palestinian return to their original homes; both proclaim that Israel must remain a Jewish state politically and demographically; both define nearly all forms of Palestinian violence as terrorism; both consider the Nazi Holocaust to be an exceptional genocide; and both deny the immorality of Israel's ethnic cleansing. The ADL, in other words, tacitly supports the same types of political violence the Kahane Movement is brave enough to own.

The ADL and Academics

Some years back, then B'nai B'rith president Seymour Reich attracted unwelcome attention when he suggested that "the Arab presence on the college campus is poisoning the minds of our young people."[51] Reich, then as now, could have been accused of incitement, for in the humanities and social sciences Arabs are remarkably underrepresented. Even if Arabs, like Jews, were overrepresented, it certainly doesn't prove intent to poison impressionable minds. But that hasn't stopped the ADL from crusading against this improbable possibility.

The ADL has a department named Campus and Higher Education Affairs. The department is involved in an array of educational and curricular matters, but its main focus is providing students with propaganda for use in the culture wars around the Israel-Palestine conflict. Its resources include *Fighting Back: A Handbook for Responding to Anti-Israel Rallies on College and University Campuses* and *Advocating for Israel: An Activist Guide*. Under the heading "Challenges on Campus," one can find information on "Anti-Israel Activity," "Anti-Semitic Speakers," "Holocaust Denial," and "Anti-Israel Divestment Campaigns." Up for target are people like Allison Weir, the Jewish proprietor of IfAmericansKnew.org, and Mazin Qumsiyeh, a Palestinian intellectual and scientist whose honorable politics cost him a job at Yale University. Problematic groups include the Council on American Islamic Relations (CAIR), the International Solidarity Movement, Al-Awda, and the US Campaign to End the Israeli Occupation. None of these groups—or, in the case of Weir and Qumsiyeh, individuals—has even a remote connection to any form of anti-Semitism, unless anti-Semitism is defined as opposition to Israel's occupation of Palestinian land, a definition the ADL leaves us no choice but to infer even if it refuses to profess it directly. The International Solidarity Movement and the US Campaign are well represented by Jewish members and leaders.

The ADL raves about its work with campus leaders and law enforcement on various educational programs. The nature of this work has been troublesome, however. According to Matt Isaacs, "The ADL has a history of making blacklists that do, in fact, attack legitimate schools of thought with a sledgehammer."[52] Isaacs continues,

> In the early 1980s, for example, records show the organization circulated through college campuses a confidential list

of pro-Arab sympathizers "who use their anti-Zionism as a guise for their deeply felt anti-Semitism." The report contained the names of respected professors from Georgetown University, Columbia University, and the University of California at Berkeley, among others, who had criticized Israel for its invasion of Lebanon. When the Middle East Studies Association discovered the document, and called for the ADL to disown it, a high-ranking ADL official was quoted in the *New York Times* blaming it on an "overly zealous student volunteer."[53]

Noam Chomsky alone amassed a 150-page dossier. Upon receipt of the dossier, Chomsky observed, "It's hard to nail this stuff down in a court of law, but it's clear they essentially have spies in classrooms who take notes and send them to the ADL and other organizations. . . . The groups then compile dossiers they can use to condemn, attack or remove faculty members. They're like J. Edgar Hoover's files. It's kind of gutter stuff."[54] These sorts of items do not usually make their way onto the ADL's website. Instead, the ADL speaks obliquely of combating hate on campus and promoting responsible curricula, but basic inquiry illustrates that spying and intimidation are central to the ADL's strategy.

In 2009, for example, the ADL went after University of California–Santa Barbara sociology professor William Robinson for supposed acts of anti-Semitism, but as of this writing nothing about that effort has appeared on the ADL website beyond a letter by ADL Santa Barbara regional director Cyndi Silverman reprinted from the *Santa Barbara News-Press*. Silverman declares that the "issue is not academic freedom. We believe the issue is one of intimidation of students and the abuse of university communications to promote one's personal opinion."[55] No matter how much Silverman insists otherwise, the issue is precisely about academic freedom. In January 2009, Robinson circulated some news items to a course e-mail list that two students found objectionable. The news items were critical of Israel's then ongoing siege of Gaza, which angered two students, unbeknownst to Robinson. Shortly thereafter, Robinson received a letter from Silverman accusing him of crossing "the line well beyond legitimate criticism of Israel" and likely violating "numerous parts of the University of Santa Barbara

Faculty Code of Conduct."[56] The two students also wrote letters of complaint whose charges reproduced Silverman's, an unsurprising correlation because the students had approached the ADL about their displeasure.

What is particularly disturbing about Robinson's situation is the level of administrative access the ADL has been granted at UCSB. Foxman himself traveled to UCSB, where he was given an audience with "about a dozen faculty members and university officials, including Vice Chancellor for Student Affairs Michael Young and the executive dean of the College of Letters and Science, David B. Marshall."[57] According to Harold Marcuse, a history professor whose public testimony about the meeting brought to light something that would otherwise have remained unknown, "When the meeting started, Foxman quickly launched into what I would call a rant about what he said was an anti-Semitic email that professor Robinson sent to his class."[58] Foxman wasn't finished: the Committee to Defend Academic Freedom at UCSB recounts that "during Foxman's presentation and the ensuing discussion, Foxman demanded that Robinson be investigated for introducing materials critical of Israeli state policies in a course on globalization in January."[59] Information about Foxman's visit to UCSB is nowhere to be found in the ADL's promotional literature. Such news might compel people, supporters of the ADL and otherwise, to question why the public face of a civil rights organization was secretly pressuring university officials to curtail a professor's civil rights because that professor was critical of Israeli state policies.

University of California–Davis professor Sunaina Maira has had a few encounters with the ADL. The Bay Area regional office has complained to Maira's department about speakers she has hosted and activities she has participated in or supported. Maira explains that "the ADL has successfully concealed its pro-Israel agenda and role in stifling any criticism of Israel behind its work of (selectively) building alliances with other communities to combat discrimination while propagating a Zionist agenda. Thus many people in these communities are not aware that the ADL also proactively targets scholars who dare to criticize Israeli policies and engages in campaigns in harassment and intimidation."[60] For the sake of transparency I should note that I have had a minor altercation with the ADL. The head of its Denver regional office, Amy

Stein, attended a talk I gave in Boulder in 2008 and wrote a letter to my sponsors without my knowledge impugning me for noting the ADL's use of anti-Semitism as a way to suppress criticism of Israel.

This kind of activity is not isolated. The ADL has a long history of creating and circulating lists of "black demagogues" and "pro-Arab propagandists." It also works outside the academy on a variety of issues amenable to state repression. Isaacs reveals that "in 1993, a longtime ADL investigator admitted to working with a member of the San Francisco Police Department to illegally gather information on almost 10,000 people, including members of socialist, labor, and anti-apartheid groups."[61] Groups the ADL has illegally surveyed include the NAACP, Farm Workers Union, the Arab-American Anti-Discrimination Committee (ADC), National Lawyers Guild, the American Indian Movement (AIM), and the United Auto Workers. Beyond the sheer number of people the ADL has monitored, what stands out most is the ideological diversity of those the ADL deems perilous. All these groups have one characteristic in common: each is a perceived threat to elite interests in either Israel or the United States. The ADL isn't acting irrationally: it is profoundly conjoined to the elite interests under attack by activists of a variety of ideological worldviews. In addition to engaging in longtime spying, the ADL is firmly opposed to affirmative action; is adamantly pro-war; and, like Israel, sided with apartheid forces in South Africa. The ADL is essentially a state policing apparatus pretending to be a civil rights organization.

The ADL and the Armenian Genocide

People weak and strong have been attempting to derail the ADL's tactics for decades, but it took a small but committed group of Armenian Americans in 2007 to succeed. This group managed to generate negative PR for the ADL and forced it to stand down from one of its major policy positions, denial of Turkey's 1915–1917 genocide against Armenians. It all happened with ironic pizzazz: members of the Armenian community of Watertown, Massachusetts, protested the sponsorship by the ADL of Watertown's school program No Place for Hate. A brouhaha ensued, generating national exposure, with the Armenian American community, organized under the group No Place for Denial (the Anti-Denial League), banishing No Place for Hate from Watertown and forcing the ADL to reluctantly affirm (sort of) the Armenian genocide.

The Armenian genocide generates much less attention in the United States than the Nazi Holocaust, in part because it was a civilized Western power that perpetrated the Nazi Holocaust and in part because groups like the ADL refuse to commemorate any genocide other than the Nazi Holocaust (and then the ADL only recognizes its Jewish victims, regularly ignoring the mass killing of Roma, the disabled, homosexuals, and others who existed on the wrong side of Hitler's eugenics). Serious historians agree that the massacre of Armenians by Ottoman Turks, which included rampant arrests and forced displacements, meets the legal and political definition of genocide.[62] To question whether the death of 1.5 million Armenians is a genocide, then, is to engage in highly dubious remonstration (what the sane call "moral sophism"). Neither Turkey nor the United States has recognized the genocide of Armenians. Israel hasn't, either, which is why the ADL so long denied it (and arguably continues to deny it). These denials illuminate the dynamic nature of genocide. They are not events rooted in history that we can recover through voice and memory. They are evolving and contested phenomena that energize political identities and supplement economic interests.

When people in Watertown decided to contest the presence of the ADL in the town's educational program, they weren't simply protesting hypocrisy; they were also asserting their political and ethnic identities as members of a community who refuse to have their history stolen by those who have already commodified the act of remembrance. It is important to continue thinking about the role of power in the exhibition of memory and the access to exposition. In capitalist societies, the ability to tell a collective story is tied to economic factors that hierarchize suffering based on its social capital and its political uses in the present. The Nazi Holocaust creates a strong economic market through its use by the film and publishing industries. Part of its economic success has been the acknowledgment by the world of its horrors. Part of its economic success has been its invention as exceptional and unsurpassed evil, a formulation that absolves Western consumers of the ongoing violence in which we are complicit and that devalues the horrible colonial violence in which genocide was first practiced, actualizing the racialist conditions for the Nazi Holocaust. There are deeply troublesome moral implications with this method of remembrance.

Its most troublesome implication is a disavowal of the genocidal violence underlying the creation of the United States, toward both African slaves and their descendants and hundreds of indigenous nations. The problem with much genocide remembrance, particularly of the Nazi Holocaust, is that it happens in isolation from relevant historical events and, worse, from their ongoing consequences in international affairs. It's well and good to remember and commemorate a genocide, but how useful is it if that genocide is treated as an exceptional horror that warrants a special place in history? It's not very useful at all if a corresponding genocide is taking place, as with Palestinians at the hands of Israel. It achieves the status of depraved if the commemorated genocide is actively used in the service of the corresponding genocide. To conceptualize genocide as an unusually malicious event rooted in a particular history doesn't allow us to integrate the world's continual bloodshed into a type of comprehensive understanding that enables us to be effectively resistant. The ADL doesn't desire this sort of result; it has made it clear that it is interested primarily in Israel's well-being. Its method of commemorating the Nazi Holocaust is therefore lewd and coercive.

The situation in Watertown quickly became ugly, with the ADL refusing to acknowledge the Armenian genocide and swiftly firing its New England regional director, Andrew H. Tarsy, when he disapproved publicly of that refusal.[63] When the negative PR reached an unprecedented level, the ADL issued a derogated acknowledgment of the Armenian genocide. Its only ungrudging lines are also its most disingenuous:

> We [the ADL] have never negated but have always described the painful events of 1915–1918 perpetrated by the Ottoman Empire against the Armenians as massacres and atrocities. On reflection, we have come to share the view of Henry Morgenthau, Sr. that the consequences of those actions were indeed tantamount to genocide. If the word genocide had existed then, they would have called it genocide.[64]

Earlier in the statement, the ADL refers to the genocide as "the Turkish-Armenian issue," a much more forthright descriptor than the equivocal phrase "tantamount to genocide," a noncommittal interpretation that the ADL nevertheless disowns, ascribing it instead to Henry Morgenthau Sr., whose relevance to the matter is a mystery. It is also interesting to see how adeptly the ADL squirms out of accepting any responsibility in its denial of the Armenian genocide. By explaining obliquely that "they would have called it genocide" had the word existed "back then," the ADL actually prolongs its denial. We are never made to understand to whom "they" refers. Indeed, people have been calling Turkey's actions a genocide for many decades now. The ADL appears to want applause for reluctantly admitting to the existence of a historical phenomenon on which scholars have long reached a consensus even though it frames its halfhearted acknowledgment with renewed denial.

Just because the ADL was forced away from its official genocide denial doesn't mean that the ADL is prepared to actually do anything that might promote healing or prevent future atrocities. "Having said that," the statement ends, "we continue to firmly believe that a Congressional resolution on such matters is a counterproductive diversion and will not foster reconciliation between Turks and Armenians and may put at risk the Turkish Jewish community and the important multilateral relationship between Turkey, Israel, and the United States."[65] The ADL is decent enough here to reveal why it has been eager to maintain its denial of genocide: it privileges the interests of Israel over all other considerations, including the advancement of its sacrosanct mission to memorialize and counteract genocide. The ADL has yet to affirm the existence of genocidal violence against American, Palestinians, Iraqis, Kurds, and black South Africans, violence in which it is either complicit or that it actively fosters. Its qualification about opposing the "counterproductive diversion" of formally recognizing the Armenian genocide might not be the most idiotic utterance, but it certainly is in contention for the most hypocritical or insensitive.

Its primary competition is a statement Foxman made to the *Forward*: "I didn't make a mistake [in denying the Armenian genocide]. . . . No Armenian lives are under threat today or in danger. Israel is under threat and in danger, and a relationship between Israel and Turkey is vital and critical, so yeah, I have to weigh [that]."[66] Foxman's statement brilliantly illuminates the ADL's strategic and rhetorical methodologies: proffer completely indemonstrable or patently false assertions, devalue all lives that aren't Jewish, accommodate realpolitik and ignore moral responsibility, and lie and equivocate brazenly. Do it all for Israel.

The Verdict

I have amassed a body of evidence that illustrates profound and systematic hypocrisy and the promotion of hateful ideologies by the ADL. But do these facts render the ADL a hate group? It is difficult to answer this question definitively because we must first consider which criteria we will use to define a hate group. There are no systematic criteria in existence on which analysts can rely. The U.S. government does not have a formal definition of hate group (even if it did, it may not be prudent to unthinkingly accept it). There are no criteria employed by various worldwide bodies such as the UN or Amnesty International. Different organizations and nongovernmental organizations use their own definitions; no one set of criteria is standard.

Therefore, I do not try to define the ADL as a hate group. I instead argue that, according to its own public criteria, the ADL should classify itself as a hate group. It is guilty of the same behavior by which it implicates those it classifies as hate groups. Here are the primary traits by which the ADL defines a hate group:

- The group's ideologies and activities perpetuate extremism and hatred.
- It adheres to a radical ideology or religious belief.
- It has pent-up anger and frustration.
- Its beliefs can lead to violent acts or terrorism.
- It is willing to use violence to upset the status quo.
- Its actions can affect entire communities, or even nations.
- It can believe in racial superiority.
- It is willing to break the law and to use violence to achieve its goals.
- It seeks to harm perceived enemies or to undermine American democracy.
- It engages in systematic Holocaust denial.

I have not rendered these criteria in my own words; they are paraphrased closely from the ADL's "Extremism in America."[67] The

ADL doesn't offer an explicit list of criteria, but these are the traits it identifies in the database. Let's look at each criterion individually and match it against the ADL's own actions and beliefs. **1. The group's ideologies and activities perpetuate extremism and hatred.** The ADL easily fits this criterion. Its unwavering support of Israel is my primary reason for this judgment. However, it needs to be made clear that it is not support of Israel in the abstract that is the main problem (though such support is nonetheless problematic); it is the ADL's ardent support of Israel's hard-line state policies that consign it to the perpetuation of extremism and hatred. The ADL does not speak against any official Israeli state policy. As a result, it becomes an active supporter of garrison settlement, the murder of civilians, religious chauvinism, home demolition, diplomatic malfeasance, the suppression of dissent, legal segregation, torture, widespread violation of international law, ethnonationalism, and chemical warfare. **Verdict: Yes.**

2. It adheres to a radical ideology or religious belief. The ADL fits this criterion if we conceptualize Zionism as a radical ideology or religious belief. This proposition in turn is based on how we choose to define "radical." Zionism is not radical in the sense of progressive or transformative politics, but it is radical using a classic definition, as something beyond the pale of decent behavior or something unseemly, inappropriate, or unbefitting of proper conduct. All of these valuations are fluid, however, and so it is difficult to conjoin them with a particular ideology. I view Zionism as radical in that it occupies a distinctly minority position in world opinion, but I hesitate to use this fact as an antecedent to concrete judgment if only because it is never a good idea to use a minority position to determine the worthiness of an idea (even if it is an appropriate determinant when it comes to Zionism). **Verdict: Indeterminate.**

3. It has pent-up anger and frustration. Likely the ADL brain trust is afflicted with these problems, but it is impossible to prove in almost any situation, pertaining to any organization. This criterion is thoroughly stupid, then. It is also one of the ADL's favorites. **Verdict: No.**

4. Its beliefs can lead to violent acts or terrorism. It would be extremely difficult to prove that the ADL's beliefs, which are exceedingly violent, lead to actual violence. (The same is true of most neo-Nazi outfits.) It would be extremely difficult to prove such an assertion in almost any case; the interrelationship of violence and belief is more complex than ADL cogitation is able to accommodate. However, it is undeniable that the ADL openly supports acts that are violent and terroristic, not only those perpetrated by Israel, but also by the American military in Iraq, Afghanistan, and Latin America. In this sense, the ADL is embroiled in violence and terrorism in profound and complicated ways, even if the causality of what it supports and the outcomes of that support are difficult to illustrate definitively. **Verdict: Yes.**

5. **It is willing to use violence to upset the status quo.** This too is a complicated criterion in that the ADL in so many ways represents the American status quo, which is endemically violent. The ADL is also a mouthpiece of the equally violent Israeli status quo. We can surmise that if the status quo in the United States were to become unfavorable to Israel, the ADL would be willing to do anything to upset it. We cannot prove this suspicion, however. **Verdict: Indeterminate.**

6. **Its actions can affect entire communities, or even nations.** That the ADL's actions can do these things is eminently demonstrable, especially if the nation in question is Palestine. **Verdict: Yes.**

7. **It can believe in racial superiority.** The ADL does not speak of Arabs and Jews using the language of race, which it reserves (appropriately) for its critique of neo-Nazis and other white supremacists, for whom such language is imperative. But I argue that the ADL adheres clearly to the spirit of this criterion, to its inherent moral reproach. Even if the language differs, the ADL visibly supports a distinct form of ethnonationalism, which is evident in Foxman's statement about the Armenian holocaust, previously quoted, and in the ADL's core belief that Israel must remain a Jewish-majority state—that is, a state predicated explicitly on racialist policy, and a state whose demography will be regulated on the basis of biological criteria. The ADL may not believe in the superiority of Jews, but it openly believes in the need for Jews to retain access to political and economic privileges that is superior to other ethnic groups' access. **Verdict: Yes.**

8. **It is willing to break the law and to use violence to achieve its goals.** Only the ADL's leaders can say with certainty what they are willing to do to achieve their goals. We can observe that the ADL

is willing to lobby for the ratification or revocation of laws that will help it achieve its goals, but it hasn't yet been shuttered by the government for illegal activities, probably because it provides intelligence to law enforcement agencies. **Verdict: No.**

9. It seeks to harm perceived enemies or to undermine American democracy. This criterion is tricky because it assumes that American democracy is a force of exclusive good, a notion contravened by its domestic and international record. We also need to think about the different ways that "harm" can be defined. The ADL, like all Zionist lobbies, has shown a willingness to put Israel's interests ahead of the United States', which can reasonably be conceptualized as a way of at least tacitly undermining American democracy. And it has no problem attacking its enemies. In fact, the ADL threatens its enemies' professional and economic safety. It spies on fellow citizens. It lobbies to remove professors from their jobs, thus imperiling their livelihoods. The ADL's many enemies would all probably say they felt harmed by their unfortunate luck in being targeted by one of the most vindictive civil rights groups currently operating in the United States. **Verdict: Yes.**

10. It engages in systematic holocaust denial. The ADL is thoroughly dedicated to educating people about the Nazi Holocaust and sponsoring numerous types of memorialization. It might be surprising, then, that this criterion is the one that can most trenchantly be applied to the ADL. Its longstanding formal policy of denying the Armenian genocide is proof enough. Yet even after a devastating PR campaign against the ADL pushed it to the brink of wholesale delegitimization, the ADL ostensibly acknowledged the Armenian genocide without actually stating unambiguously that the subject of its acknowledgment was genocide. Even after its disclaimed admission, the ADL has actively blocked any action that might allow the descendents of the Armenian genocide to move forward through admission and reconciliation. The ADL is opposed only to genocidal acts that can somehow be of use to Israel. **Verdict: Yes.**

Of the ten criteria the ADL advances about the potential traits of a hate group, it acutely matches six of them and resembles two others. I cannot say conclusively that these factors make the ADL a hate group, but it is indisputable that the ADL satisfies its own conception of a hate group. The ADL works hard to attach all of its initiatives to its commitment to Israel. From a philosophical and ethical standpoint, this move discredits all of those efforts because Israel is a settler colonial nation whose core state ideologies and jurisprudence are unavoidably racist. More generally, when a civil rights group works within apparatuses of state power and promotes responsible policing as a form of justice, it will inevitably betray whatever humanistic principles it broadcasts. That the ADL invests so much time in law enforcement renders it automatically dubious. That it aggressively protects Israel from criticism renders it eminently hypocritical. On the basis of all the research I have collected, I argue that the ADL isn't fulfilling its original mission of eliminating anti-Semitism, just as noble a goal now as it was in 1913. In fact, it probably does more to foment than to contest anti-Semitism.

The ADL is not exceptional. There isn't, as most people want to believe, a large gap between a civil rights and a hate group. One of the main reasons that the two sometimes shade into one another is that the affectations of radicalism by civil rights groups often conceal an unimaginative reliance on the mechanisms of juridical intervention, which are influenced by a completely different set of goals and imperatives (those of protecting the elite). There is no good way to reconcile these divergent interests no matter how insistently civil rights groups sermonize about kinder and gentler policing techniques. Ultimately, any organization interested in real justice must be independent and contestatory. As soon as it attaches itself to an economic or political group or to a state bureaucracy it has compromised its ability to be anything more than superficially effective. Therein exists the special depravity of the ADL: it has attached itself to two different state apparatuses; rather than pretending to hold both accountable, it uses one to enlarge the other. If the ADL is the apotheosis of a civil rights group, then the many honorable targets of its invidious advocacy should be proud to call themselves uncivil.

3 Ethnonationalism as an Object of Multicultural Decorum

The Case of Cornel West and Michael Eric Dyson

The ass went looking for horns and lost his ears.

—ARABIC PROVERB

I n this chapter I examine the work of two intellectuals whose scholarship is rooted in socially liberal traditions of black Christianity. Both intellectuals, Cornel West and Michael Eric Dyson, are prolific writers and public figures. Both have produced seminal theoretical and philosophical work. Both comment frequently on issues of broad debate (using points of view considered radical by corporate media standards). And both occupy exalted positions in academe (West at Princeton and Dyson at Georgetown). The two are generally aligned politically and work within the same intellectual traditions, some of which each helped create. West and Dyson are two of this generation's most important intellectuals. Their work is wide-ranging and often intended for nonacademic readers, an admirable orientation that entails a set of special problems. One of these problems encompasses the political expectations of the audiences, which tend to be sharper and less ambivalent than those of academic readers. When it comes to the Israel-Palestine conflict, this problem is particularly acute. West and Dyson betray their deftness as critical intellectuals when they discuss the Israel-Palestine conflict in their roles as nonacademic commentators. They therefore offer interesting complexities to contemplate about the inherent problem of the public intellectual.

Cornel West and the Ethics of Faithful Equivocation

Cornel West is one of a handful of modern American intellectuals who have come to symbolize academic radicalism among popular commentators without ever actually having proposed any truly radical ideas, those that seek to dismantle rather than ameliorate structures of economic, sexual, and racial injustice. Like the vast majority of people conceptualized as public intellectuals, West did not develop his broad public appeal by espousing dangerous ideas. (The obvious exception was Edward Said, but he arguably never achieved the same level of mainstream acceptance as West.) Yet his appeal as a straw man for curmudgeonly culture warriors chafed by the supposed decay of timeless Western values indicates that West is nevertheless mildly threatening, even if he isn't really taken to task for being radical but for not being quite patriotic enough. There is one area in particular in which West's writing fails to achieve either analytical or ethical distinctiveness, thereby acting as a metonym for West's political timidity in general: the Israel-Palestine conflict, something West assesses beyond the boundaries of its own history by emphasizing multicultural American paradigms rather than revolutionary decolonial advocacy.

In speaking about the Israel-Palestine conflict, West often employs the liberal American vocabulary of tolerance and coexistence, an anomalous approach that reduces Israeli Jews and Palestinian Arabs to irrationally competing factions who merely need more open-minded dialogue rather than a significant redistribution of land ownership, natural resources, economic capital, political power, and military strength. Also to be overcome are serious restrictions on Palestinian freedom of movement, upward mobility, urban development, and access to farmland, family, education, and employment. The Israel-Palestine conflict is not the result of poor communication, religious acrimony, or cultural intolerance. These phenomena are the outcomes of foreign settlement and ethnic cleansing, not their progenitors. By emphasizing these phenomena rather than Jewish ethnonationalism, West decontextualizes the Israel-Palestine conflict from its proper origin in Zionist colonization and reifies Israel's placement in proper multicultural discourse as a legitimate exemplar of Jewish culture, worth celebration and indispensible to the adoration of diversity.

West, a dexterous intellectual, should know better than to uncritically conceptualize a nation-state as worthy of the sort of exaltation that attends cultural interchange. States are self-regulating actors whose interests cannot be detached from myriad iniquities arising from their very structure and their inescapable relationships with competing entities. As Amilcar Cabral observed, "The value of culture as an element of resistance to foreign domination lies in the fact that culture is the vigorous manifestation on the ideological or idealist plane of the physical and historical reality of the society that is dominated or to be dominated."[1] Cabral's statement urges people to identify with the cultures of resistance vis-à-vis the technocracy of the oppressive state, an appeal that is especially valuable when we think about the monotonous conflation of Jewish culture with Israeli technocracy. To perfunctorily accept Israel as a timeless and legitimate repository of Jewish culture overlooks the violence that informs its very existence. Cultural interchange, on the other hand, occurs ideally beyond the confined physical and imaginative boundaries of the nation-state.

The main problem with West's point of view on the Israel-Palestine conflict is his insistence, like that of his political collaborator Michael Lerner's, that there is an equivalence between Israel's violent actions and all forms of Palestinian resistance that in some way use physical violence. Yet the very presence of Israel is an unmistakably continuous violence; it is foolish to limit our conception of the term to actions that result in palpable harm or destruction. On the conflict, West sounds much less like the autonomous thinker he is on most issues and a bit like a sycophantic version of Lerner and other classically liberal Zionists. Even in their conversations-cum-full-on-book, *Jews and Blacks*, West constantly fails to rein in Lerner's rehearsed discourses of victimization that tacitly position Jews as eternal scapegoats of Arab and black aggression. Nearly every time West asserts a thoughtful position, he is made to moderate it or retreat from it altogether. Israel therefore becomes a protected space, able to be criticized but unable to be fundamentally challenged as a failed ethnocentric project or a deeply unjust idea. (We will encounter the same problem with Dyson.) I wish West would cancel his *Tikkun* subscription and dust off his copy of *The Wretched of the Earth*.

West discusses the Israel-Palestine conflict at length in *Democracy Matters*, noting correctly that "the roots of the conflict go back to the shadows cast by the British empire." He attributes the persistence of the conflict to a variety of factors, among them American irresponsibility, extremist Arab and Israeli leaders, oil politics, diplomatic myopia, citizen apathy, historical ignorance, arrogant [U.S.] Republicans, and tribalism and parochialism (whose advocates West never reveals). Nowhere does he identify the conflict's most vexing problem: Zionism. I am aware that Zionism is not consistent philosophically, temporally, and politically. I deploy the term here to denote its most basic feature, the notion, in whatever form, that Israel should exist as a Jewish nation-state culturally and demographically, an entity to which Jews anywhere in the world have access (a privilege withheld from the native Palestinians). This unifying attribute of Zionist thought reinforces the ethnocentric outlook that inspired settler colonization in Palestine, without which there would have been no conflict and without whose continuation the conflict would have long ago ceased. West is not merely negligent by ignoring the turpitude of Zionism; in so doing, he becomes complicit in the suffering it produces.

West's emphasis on moral equivalency arises in the framework of such negligence. West condemns "zealously driven power players, be they in the U.S. government, Islamic states, or Israel."[2] Accordingly, "at the moment both Israel and the Arab world are currently under the thrall of extremist thinkers and power players."[3] Regarding the Israelis and Palestinians specifically, he decries their "arrogant and stubborn leaders"[4] and mourns the "paranoia [that] has been used by the nihilistic xenophobes on both sides."[5] Reading *Democracy Matters*, one gets the impression that the Israel-Palestine conflict is an inexplicable misunderstanding nourished by a proportional number of autocrats, nihilists, and extremists in Israel and the Arab World. West's understanding of settler colonization is subordinate to his insistence that the conflict can be resolved through earnest multicultural dialogue. This argument imposes a liberal American paradigm of tolerance on a decidedly intolerable situation and it fails to properly acknowledge the tremendous power differential between Palestinian Arabs and Israeli Jews.

Equally alarming is West's distorted historical perspective, one that has achieved the status of authentic in most American intellectual communities. Like Lerner, he saves his harshest language for Arabs:

> The barbarity of the terrorism launched against Jews in Israel first by the Arab states and now by the suicide bombers is real and should never be explained away—as the zealots on the Palestinian side do—but the dominant Jewish stance has become so hardened by the pain of this suffering, and by the feeling of being so reviled by enemies, that the Jewish community has been losing touch with its own rich prophetic tradition.[6]

If he wishes to be consistent in his ethical outlook, West should also add that in the 1950s southern whites in the United States turned fire hoses onto black children because they felt so besieged by African American demands for civil liberties; that white South Africans were terrified for their safety during the Soweto riots; and that French cynicism arises from the fact that they suffered Algerian resistance to their dream of an all-white African colony. His use of the word "barbarity" to describe Palestinian behavior is troublesome. The word conjures discourses of modernity and premodernity; it is not a word frequently used to describe Western violence, even when that violence is condemned. "Barbarity" confines Palestinians to a class of colonized subjects encompassing hundreds of years whose tactics of resistance are condemned as egregious and irrational by those in sympathy with the colonizer. By deploying the term, West makes his sympathy for Israel indubitable, whether or not that was his intent.

Beyond his ethically dangerous argument, West recycles mythologies that are empirically untrue. Jewish settlers, not Arabs, introduced terrorism to Palestine. In 1944 Menachem Begin, future prime minister of Israel, led a campaign of bombings at British police stations and tax and immigration offices.[7] In 1946 the British embassy in Rome was bombed by members of the Stern Gang, the same outfit that assassinated Lord Moyne in Cairo and, later, UN peacemaker Folke Bernadotte. The Moyne assassination was carried out under the auspices of another future Israeli prime minister,

Yitzhak Shamir. In 1948 members of Irgun and the Stern Gang slaughtered nearly two hundred civilians in the Palestinian village of Deir Yassin, a massacre the supposedly moderate Haganah militia encouraged. Such massacres occurred throughout the Galilee during 1947–1949, ultimately resulting in the expulsion of approximately seven hundred thousand Palestinians, who have never been granted any form of reentry. In 1947 Irgun members exploded a bomb from a taxi at Jerusalem's Damascus Gate, killing two British officers and eleven Palestinian civilians. A year earlier, Jewish terrorists blew up Jerusalem's King David Hotel, killing at least two hundred people (another act involving the so-called good cop Haganah).[8]

To suggest that Jewish settlers in Palestine fell victim to barbarous terrorism, as West does, entails an implicit chauvinism masquerading as learned magnanimity. Again, West ignores the matter of colonization and assesses the conflict in a vacuum, as if European Jews were somehow native to a non-European nation. (He likewise ignores the now-conclusive fact that the Israeli army was far superior to the combined Arab armies in 1948.)[9] More disturbingly, West implies that any type of moral transgression committed by Jews arises not from their own depravity but from the corrupting presence of the Palestinians. Rather than condemning the century-old dispossession of Palestinians, West mourns the decline of the "Jewish prophetic tradition," something apparently instigated by their encounter with Palestinians. In fact, West spends much of his analysis praising Judaic traditions of pacifism and introspection, which certainly exist, but mentions nothing of Palestinian intellectual and spiritual traditions, which also certainly exist (and are indivisible from those of their Jewish brethren). His constant reference to and simplification of Palestinian violence reinforces the implication that it is ultimately up to the Jews, those of a proper moral caliber, to liberate the Palestinians by saving them from barbarity. West writes from the perspective of his own intellectual and ethical influences, particularly that of the prophetic Christianity he references. He makes it obvious, despite halfhearted dissimulation to the contrary, that he sees Jews as central to that glorious tradition but imagines Arabs to exist in less sanctified spaces.

The title of the chapter in which this analysis appears, "Forging New Jewish and Islamic Democratic Identities," illuminates West's poor understanding of the Israel-Palestine conflict (or his conscious misrepresentation of it). Forging democratic identities is not a bad idea, but the lack of such identities among certain communities of Jews and Muslims (which West never identifies) has little to do with the origin and endurance of the Israel-Palestine conflict. Indeed, were the legitimate democratic will of Arab peoples to be implemented, Israel would cease to exist as a racist and imperialist state bisecting the Arab World; it would instead evolve into a space with equal rights for all of its citizens. Most opinion polls taken in the Arab World show a majority of its citizens willing to coexist with Israeli Jews as long as actual democracy prevails. A 2007 Near East Consulting poll found that 70.4 percent of Palestinians support "a one-state solution in historic Palestine where Muslims, Christians and Jews have equal rights and responsibilities."[10] Israel's own Judeocentric democratic tradition has ensured the continued displacement of Palestinians; the responsibility for ensuring justice, after all, belongs to the perpetrator of injustice. It is one of the fascinating qualities of colonization that throughout the centuries the colonized have always been much more generous to their enemies and far more open to genuine coexistence than the colonizers who exhaust their tongues preaching humanistic values to their subordinates, the same values they ceremoniously ignore.

Like other shortsighted commentators on the Israel-Palestine conflict, West delimits the history of Israeli brutality, noting that "the ugly thirty-seven-year Israeli occupation of Palestinian lands and subjugation of Palestinian peoples violate international law and any code of humanitarian ethics."[11] This claim is entirely demonstrable and West is to be commended for owning a viewpoint that is controversial despite its basis in reality. He is to be condemned, however, for forgetting (or disregarding) the ethnic cleansing that accompanied Israel's 1948 founding, as well as the malicious intentions (now well documented) of Zionist leaders during British rule. The Nazi Holocaust in Europe seems a direct antecedent to Israel's founding, but such a perception is actually more convenient than veracious: there was knowledge among the earliest Zionists that Palestine was widely inhabited, and there were plans from the outset of Zionism to rid the Promised Land of its indigenous population.[12]

West's criticism of Israel's behavior assumes that Israel was always a geopolitical entity in the image of a modern nation-state and that it has inherent value as a consciously ethnocentric (and thus exclusive) society. Both assumptions are morally dubious and intellectually pusillanimous. No rationale for Israel's existence as a timeless Jewish-majority state is free of deeply sectarian presuppositions. When transported to the Middle East, West's multicultural humanism unwittingly reveals its own illiberal anatomy, one that emphasizes abstruse idealism more than structures of injustice. But it is the structures of injustice of primary concern to the committed humanist. The strictures of political convention should never be a terminus but an occasion for vigorous inquiry. To normatize Zionism as inherently reasonable is to surrender integrity as a theorist of conscience.

Perhaps it is West's emphasis on abstruse idealism—one that manages to sound profound while performing spectacularly conventional political work—that leads him to speak in truisms and platitudes. A few passages from "Forging New Jewish and Islamic Democratic Identities" suffice to illuminate the worthlessness of West's analysis: "The recent history of prophetic American Jews questioning the myopic viewpoint and Manichean framework of this conflict is appalling";[13] "prophetic Jews are up against formidable Jewish establishmentarian forces";[14] "to erase the modern West is to ignore the dark predicament of the Islamic present";[15] "the delicate dialogue between the modern West and the Islamic world . . . should be a Socratic process of examining a rich past of cultural cross-fertilization";[16] "needless to say, the fall of any nihilistic gangster who rules with an iron hand is salutary."[17]

I suppose it is possible that West actually wants to sound as if he's a fortune cookie writer with a Ph.D. He does have a propensity for liberal bromides no matter what the topic, but in the context of the Israel-Palestine conflict this style appears especially disquieting. The metaphorical campfire he wants Jews and Palestinians to sit around might be appropriate for diversity workshops, but it is inadequate for a conflict whose main feature has been cultural genocide. West's purported evenhandedness allows him to ingratiate himself to liberal Zionists; he appears to believe that he can satisfy the fundamentally racist assumptions of the conflict's most powerful demographic but still retain his exalted position as a public intellectual of uncommon probity. It is no coincidence that liberal Zionists have decided that the height of intellectual and ethical responsibility happens to coincide with one's commitment to retaining Israel's identity as a Jewish state. This irresponsible notion of responsibility pervades liberal conversation around race and culture in the United States. West is merely a famous purveyor of a widespread problem: the tacit belief that Jews must be normatively associated with the outcome of their colonial policies rather than being held responsible for those policies according to international law. In other words, just because most Jews dislike the idea of a truly democratic state in Israel/Palestine—that is, one in which Jews don't hold the vast majority of power—it doesn't mean that such a state is inherently a bad idea. It simply means that most Jews will need to be coerced to accept a reality much fairer and ethically superior to the one they created. The Palestinians are not asking for anything other than what is already theirs and what they are entitled to according to international law. Yet these basic demands are treated by West and other responsible intellectuals as untenable and irrational. Bodies of scholarly and documentary evidence supporting Palestinian claims must be ignored in order to employ such an approach.

West does important work by bringing to wide audiences knowledge of the harshness of Palestinian life in the Occupied Territories. These positive qualities are not reason enough to absolve him of a dumbed-down perspective on the Israel-Palestine conflict, however, nor should we excuse his complicity in the process of making Israel a normative feature of multicultural celebration. Ultimately, West's responsibility, like that of any writer, is to the truth, no matter what it leads him to conclude, and not to the banalities of a supposedly tasteful ideology.

Michael Eric Dyson and the Inconvenience of Colonization

Michael Eric Dyson has become at least as well known as Cornel West. He has moved away from his earlier theoretical and philosophical work and now publishes a prolific list of trade books, many of them conversational and all of them about race in the United States. Dyson appears to spend much more time these days on punditry than on scholarship. This transition doesn't devalue his analyses, however. It illuminates a new cultural dynamic in the

United States in which black public intellectuals contribute more frequently to mainstream conversations around sensitive topics like race relations. That cultural dynamic isn't necessarily a sign of progress. In many ways, it conceals the existence of profoundly conservative assumptions in the vocabularies of racial reckoning. Dyson's popularity, like that of West's, relies largely on his intelligence and eloquence. His media ubiquity relies mainly on symbolic phenomena much larger than himself. These symbolic phenomena revolve around the spectacle of the pundit as authoritative expert. In Dyson's case, he is an authority on race and black politics, called into service whenever a legitimizing voice is required. By "legitimizing voice," I do not mean to impugn whatever politics Dyson advocates; rather, I identify his innate legitimacy for those to whom racial opining is a tricky business (in this case white media executives). The pundit plays a precise role as a spectacle in modern American cultures of mass media. He—in most cases it is a he—speaks in sound bites conducive to advertising sales, which occupy a majority of the airtime the pundit covets. He is there to help construct a market niche, not to clarify matters of vital social import. His opinions must not disrupt the sale of the advertisements themselves, which means that he cannot threaten the desirability of the advertisers' products. Race is thus automatically commodified in the United States' sites of multicultural interchange, and the pundit himself, the public face of this punctilious salesmanship, is merely a vassal of free market commerce.

I do not reduce all of Dyson's work to this process, but he participates often in it—for instance, as a talking head with his wife during the Democratic primaries of 2008, with Dyson supporting Barack Obama and his wife supporting Hillary Clinton. In less than five minutes of conversation, they would argue publicly as if engaged in a private family debate without having an opportunity to usefully analyze the inequitable structures of American electoral protocol. Instead, they attempted to re-create the discursive circus of cutesy he said/she said political-bickering-for-profit popularized by married couple James Carville and Mary Matalin. (It hardly bears pointing out that such bickering is invariably spurious.) This sort of performance reinforces the reality that political difference within the confines of corporate politics is overwhelmingly superficial, something that can itself be dramatized for profit.

Dyson's shortcomings, as so many others', are exposed by the topic of Palestine. It is not a topic that Dyson discusses frequently, and one that he almost never invokes voluntarily. However, given his widespread punditry, his viewpoint on the Israel-Palestine conflict is sometimes requested. His responses are uniformly mealy-mouthed and conciliatory. A remarkably eloquent orator and writer, Dyson somehow becomes a rhetorical cad when the issue of Palestine arises. In a 2008 interview with Amy Goodman, for instance, Dyson responded to a question about Obama's pandering to Israel:

> Yeah, well, obviously, Mr. Obama is conscious of, you know, making certain that security for Israel is paramount, for a variety of reasons too complex, all of which, to parse here. But I think that, obviously, he is conscious of the fact that Israel's place and prominence in American foreign policy is a given, and his argument to defend them is something that has been problematic to many people, as well as the fact that the difficulty of having balanced discourse, rhetoric and dialogue in America about Palestine and Israel and the relationship between those two competing forces in that region, and Israel's security, as well as Palestine's—the Palestinians' security in that area, it's a very [difficult] and tricky way.[18]

Dyson's response is worse than Cornel West's support of Israeli colonization. I do not offer this judgment on the basis of the content or tone of his response to Goodman. I base it on the more abstract factor of audacity: West is at least unafraid to voice his beliefs, however disquieting they are. I would rather listen to an intellectual with an opinion than one who can't even bring himself to assume the default position of state fascism. I have attempted repeatedly to glean some sort of meaning from Dyson's statement, but without success. As best as I can figure, he is attempting to say that Obama's support of Israel is objectionable but inevitable and therefore excusable.

If this is indeed Dyson's presumption—and we have no choice but to make an inference here—he is not only morally capricious but consigned to indemonstrable speculation. It is something of a truism that aspiring politicians must become sycophantic Zionists, or at least pretend to be one, but that truism buttresses anti-Semitic conspiracies of Jewish power and has no basis in actual political history; just because politicians have followed this tactic almost uniformly does not mean that the tactic is inherently judicious. It simply illustrates that Israel is a crucial element of the structures of elite industry whose interests politicians in capitalist societies are obliged to serve. But it does not illustrate that Israel warrants a special adulation in the political servicing of that industry. When it is provided with special adulation by politicians like Obama, it is perfectly reasonable for intellectuals like Dyson to provide condemnation in return. Support for Israel necessarily precludes one from legitimate access to a progressive identity. By forgiving Obama of his approval—or, less charitably, encouragement—of Israeli ethnic cleansing, Dyson establishes complicity in politics that deeply belie his progressive commitments. The only point of opposition Dyson offers, after all, is presented nondescriptly as "problematic" and is passively attributed to "many people," none of whom Dyson identifies.

His performance on *Democracy Now!* is not an anomaly. His 2007 book *Debating Race* contains some evasions reminiscent of his *Democracy Now!* appearance. The book contains transcripts of many of Dyson's public appearances, sometimes alone and at other times with fellow speakers (Cornel West, for example). Dyson's punditry is on display in *Debating Race*, which includes some of his corporate media experiences. All in all, the book has a diverse range of conversation. As usual, Dyson is engaging and intelligent. He proffers surprising viewpoints and consistently has interesting things to say about subjects both popular and scholarly. Dyson's range of knowledge is impressive, his eloquence enviable. He seems to have a natural knack for performance. He is by turns stubborn and sycophantic. He also shows himself to be a shrewd self-promoter. He praises Star Jones, formerly of the ABC talk show *The View*, in his book *Why I Love Black Women* and earned himself an invitation to appear on the highly rated program. Jones tells Dyson, "You gave me a big wet kiss in that book," to which Dyson responds, "I'll tell you, I just love you. And as my wife understands, I'm deeply and profoundly attracted to you as a beautiful black woman, and as a woman who represents so much that's positive in our history."[19] In his introductory paragraph to the transcript, Dyson implies that his appearance on the program might have played a role in Jones's subsequent dismissal.[20] Here we have Dyson the spectacle, attempting to squeeze his intellectual pedigree into a program that is formatted specifically to avoid critical discussion of serious issues. In these spaces, conversation about American racism is discouraged. Mention of Palestine is strictly verboten. These demands travel. Even in his less regulated public appearances at universities and public spaces, where these demands are much less explicit, Dyson usually complies with them. His forum with Cornel West is especially interesting. An audience member assesses the applicability of liberation theology to African Americans, focusing on the "comparison between African Americans in America and the religious standpoint of the children of Israel in Egypt being in bondage," and then asks, "Is there a future for us somewhere outside America?"[21] The question is apt historically and complex morally, one that has fascinated thinkers like Marcus Garvey and Malcolm X, and one that some scholars, such as Robert Warrior, have rejected as an inappropriate model for American Indian liberation.[22]

Like Warrior, West rejects the liberation theology model for African Americans, noting, "You can't just show up when somebody else is already there," which happened not only in modern Palestine, but also in ancient Canaan, the basis for Warrior's rejection of American Indian identification with the Israelites (he urges identification with the indigenous Canaanites of Old Testament misfortune instead).[23] West elaborates on his wariness of the Old Testament model of liberation: "We got to crawl right down the Middle East with Jewish brothers and sisters. They get trashed like dogs and cockroaches by that vicious Hitler. What did they do? They got to jump out the burning buildings of Europe. They had no choice. But what'd they do? They land on the backs of some Arabs."[24] West's analysis is morally sound but nevertheless problematic. It is a common mistake to conceptualize Zionism as a response to the Holocaust. While Zionism is at least in part a response to European anti-Semitism, it is an ethnonationalist movement that originated in the late nineteenth century, well before the rise of Nazism. By the time Hitler had ascended to power, Jewish settlers in Palestine were numerous and engaged in strategies of terrorist violence. It is problematic for West to associate Israel's creation with the Holocaust because that gives the Yishuv (the pre-1948 Jewish community in Palestine) a free pass for the comprehensive ethnic cleansing they carefully planned and executed upon Israel's founding. Jews might not have had a choice but to abandon the burning buildings of Europe, but they had a choice in how they would come to treat the Palestinians. And they certainly have a choice in how they treat Palestinians right now, seventy years after the Holocaust. West has entangled himself in the contradictory dialectic between liberation and oppression, whose primary contradiction arises from the application of liberationist paradigms to the structure of the modern nation-state. The modern nation-state does not provide comprehensive liberation; it is fundamentally built on exclusions. Jewish liberation and Jewish nationhood are not coterminous desires. In any case, Jewish nationhood through the exclusionary movement of Zionism has had disastrous consequences.

Of special interest is Dyson's response to West's commendable analysis: "I'll just catch up on the next one."[25] While this might be dismissed as a typical throwaway comment of no significance, it actually accords with Dyson's avoidance and evasiveness when it comes to Palestine, as we saw in his *Democracy Now!* commentary. (Every good liberal aspiring to be the next Rachel Maddow knows that anything can be criticized except Israel.) Elsewhere in *Debating Race*, Palestine comes up. In a conversation with Elliot A. Ratzman of *HEEB* magazine, Ratzman asks a direct question to Dyson about using history to rationalize injustice against Palestinians. I quote an excerpt of Dyson's response at length:

> Now, I'm not against a kind of Foucaultian understanding versus a Weberian conception—Max Weber located power in hierarchy, rationalization, and authority, whereas Foucault said, "Yeah, but power breaks out everywhere." Foucault recognized that there are ways in which people who are powerless compete with one another over scarce resources of legitimacy, or over self-definition on a limited political terrain. I'm down with both of those. I'm Weberian *and* Foucaultian at that level. But I don't think that an empirically abstract Foucaultian conception of power would yield much in benefit to those who are trying to figure out

the next move in the Palestinian-Israeli dialogue and struggle for liberation.[26]

A bit later, Dyson explains,

> To talk about the environment within which certain things develop is not to avoid the issue of responsibility. It is simply to give a scheme of explanation a coherent expression among people who may have competing moral ideals. Because when you talk about Palestinians and Jews, for instance, you're talking about Thomas Kuhn's conception of incommensurable vocabularies. Are we really speaking about different ways of viewing the world? These might be different cosmologies at stake—it's not just different languages and different understandings, but these are different peoples constituted by different histories who have almost incoherent moral vocabularies—at least to each other—to express what they're doing. Intifada meets Prophetic Tradition.[27]

Dyson gives us much to consider, through both vagueness and circumvention. The first problem with his analysis is that he never identifies who is struggling for liberation and against whom this unnamed group is directing its struggle. One without any knowledge of the Israel-Palestine conflict would have absolutely no idea that Israel is a colonial power after reading this interview. Dyson is vague in other ways. He tries to preempt criticism that he is avoiding responsibility, but he never provides a definition of responsibility, a notoriously contested term. I too have no foolproof definition of the term, and yet I am thoroughly convinced that avoiding responsibility is precisely what Dyson is doing. For instance, the Israel-Palestine conflict has very little to do with "competing moral ideals." It has to do with the settlement by foreign Jews of Palestinian land—in other words, with colonization and resistance. Dyson may as well attribute the Jim Crow American south and France's usurpation of Algeria to "competing moral ideals." Dyson also develops the annoying habit of concealing his moral cowardice with philosophical gibberish. The Israel-Palestine conflict cannot be reduced to "Kuhn's conception of incommensurable vocabularies"—an idea Dyson completely misunderstands, anyway—and

Zionism has nothing to do with the Jewish prophetic tradition. To conflate the two is actually an insult to the prophetic tradition, an intellectual and spiritual heritage that eschews injustice; at least West, whatever his imperfections, knows how to deploy the term correctly. Dyson's most egregious evasion is conceptualizing the Israel-Palestine conflict as a deep but innocent misunderstanding. His focus on "incoherent moral vocabularies" reflects a moral incoherence on his part that is utterly damning. Perhaps Zionists have difficulty expressing to Palestinians what they are doing, but the Palestinians have absolutely no problem speaking to Israel and its Western sponsors with a cocksure moral vocabulary.

I would not use the word "cowardice" to describe Dyson's approach to the Israel-Palestine conflict if the quotations I have provided represented only one instance of his evasiveness. Unfortunately, they do not. In dialogue with another American Jew, the New Age spiritualist Marianne Williamson, an audience member asks about the validity of the oft-repeated charge that Zionism is racism. The response gets off to an interesting start:

> DYSON: That's a wide open question. I'm going to try to take a stab at it, and I know Marianne—
> WILLIAMSON: "I know a Jewish woman is standing right next to me while I do it."
> DYSON: My homegirl whom I love. [*Laughter*][28]

Williamson's response is supposed to be humorous, but it is clear that she points out her religious background as if to warn Dyson not to get too slaphappy in his criticism of Zionism. Dyson heeds the warning:

> I think Zionism has a complex history. It has some negative connotations, as Black Nationalism has, and it has some edifying ones, as Black Nationalism has. Any nationalism is suspect to me, as well as Americanism. Right? That's why, after 9/11, I made a distinction between patriotism and nationalism. Patriotism is the crucial affirmation of one's country in light of its best values. Nationalism is the support of one's nation, right or wrong. I can't go with that. No "ism" deserves our uncritical support—black, brown,

red, yellow, Jewish, Muslim, or whatever. The problem is fundamentalism. Fundamentalisms go in any religion, masquerade as any politics, masquerade in any ideology. I think we need to be critical of Israel and not be called anti-Semitic. And we should be critical of Palestine and not be called anti-Arab. Like we can be critical of African American people, and disagree with them, and not be called racist. We have to have an open conversation where the dialogue is aboveboard.[29]

Dyson's response is little more than elaborate cant. He speaks in the tired platitudes of a white intellectual trying to prove to a skeptical black audience that he isn't really racist. He avoids the question of Zionism and racism altogether and reduces Zionism to a participant in a multiethnic Rolodex of mediocre but inherently valuable ideas. His distinction between patriotism and nationalism is fatuous and contributes nothing to our understanding of the uses of power in both patriotism and nationalism.

Williamson then coerces Dyson into a specific answer again by asking, "I had heard so many people talking about Zionism like it's inherently a racist concept. And I don't see that. Do you, Michael?"[30] Dyson obediently responds, "No, I don't. Look, the existence of Israel is an idea, as Victor Hugo said, whose time had already come long before it was even established. So I am in no way critical of the establishment of a homeland for Jews."[31] Once again, Dyson flashes his habit of name-dropping in order to contextualize a cliché, in this case Victor Hugo, who I'm pretty certain never had anything to say about the existence of Israel (Hugo died in 1885). If the Palestinians weren't dying en masse and living under a brutal military occupation, there would be some humor to the spectacle of Dyson waxing philosophical about his dislike of nationalism and then less than a minute later proclaiming, "I am in no way critical of the establishment of a homeland for Jews." Dyson claims to eschew nationalism, but he reinforces the Eurocentric nation-state model of liberation. The idea of a Jewish nation, or of a Jewish homeland, is worth moral and philosophical consideration. But the idea of a Jewish state, as dictated by Zionism, is quite another proposition. It is impossible to be morally consistent in eschewing nationalism while supporting Zionism.

When Williamson announces that Zionism cannot ever be equated with injustice, the questioner notes, "The average layperson does not know all these deep things like you do," repeating a sentiment she had expressed a few times already.[32] The questioner is surely being too polite, for the irony of this conversation is that it quickly becomes clear that she, the layperson, is the only one among the three who has anything worthwhile to say. Dyson is too busy basking in the adulation that attends his dutifulness to comment further: "one of the reasons I like Michael Dyson so much . . ."; "that's why I think Michael is so important"; "that's why we're interested in bringing people like Michael here."[33]

Debating Race illuminates how the economics of comment interact with capitalist structures of distribution. To speak of an economics of comment may seem strange, but the modes of delivering information in a capitalist society can never be totally neutral or autonomous. They are confined to a dialectic between what the elite deem the national interest (a reflection of their own interests) and the processes by which information is concentrated, interpreted, and disseminated. In other words, what we are drawn to is often chosen for us, though we fool ourselves into believing the myth of consumer agency; in reality, our choices merely evince the rational pursuit of self-interest dictated by a system of personal rewards. This reward system reproduces any nation's discursive interpretation of its geopolitical engagements, particularly if those engagements are colonial, as are the United States' and Israel's. In this schema, accessibility is usually based not on merit but on agreeability. Information is concentrated around particular modes of corporate welfare. It is disseminated by degrees of proximity to corporate interests. While the Internet has been something of a democratic equalizer, the majority of mass communications and the entirety of pundit culture are still structured around the reward of complaisance. Information rarely reaches consumers unfiltered.

It is in the context of punditry and its corporate lexicon that personal branding most commonly occurs. An entire class of public intellectuals has created individual brand recognition: Alan Dershowitz, as an Israeli apologist; Henry Louis Gates Jr., as a nonpolitical patron of African American culture; Bernard-Henri Levy, as the rare French admirer of America; Todd Gitlin, as the curmudgeonly pragmatist. Dyson's pundit brand is that of the safe black radical, the intellectual who can provide a credible black voice that is appealing to liberal white Americans and completely unthreatening to Zionists. Dyson's popular work illustrates that he is extremely careful to brand himself as a radical while speaking as though a classic liberal whose discourse will not challenge entrenched centers of power. His failure to adequately criticize Zionism prevents him from developing the type of comprehensive humanism so diligently constructed in his pundit brand. For Dyson, the colonization of Palestine is not a pressing moral issue; it is simply an inconvenience. In the economics of comment, the Palestinians are a penny stock.

Debating Race has twenty-seven chapters. Not one Palestinian voice can be found in them, or a single Arab, or a single Muslim. I argue that these omissions are indefensible for a scholar who fancies himself a champion of multicultural dialogue. Dyson has no obligation to include such voices, but he confers to himself a type of responsibility that is unfulfilled by his failure to engage them. It is not just Debating Race that is up for criticism. In his rehearsed work, Dyson rarely mentions Palestine, part of a long pattern of evasion when it comes to Israeli ethnic cleansing. I do not argue that Dyson or anybody else is required to condemn Israel or discuss Palestine. But when Dyson is asked to condemn Israel or discuss Palestine, and then fancies himself an authority on the subject, he should speak as a committed public intellectual rather than as a corporatized pundit. In any case, if a person wants to know Dyson's opinion on the Israel-Palestine conflict, there is no need to read Dyson. That person need merely read Marianne Williamson instead.

The Problem of the Public Intellectual

Cornel West and Michael Eric Dyson show that there can come a point when a public intellectual becomes too public—that is to say, too entrenched in the information cycles of capitalist media. This is the main problem of the public intellectual: having to work within a system in which public life is indivisible from the abetment of norms against which the intellectual should stand. Today, the intellectual is tasked with exploring spaces that are untraditionally public, available through the possibilities begotten by alternative media. I argue that in many ways the concept of the public intellectual is antiquated, or becoming that way; it may be more useful to think about a scholar engaging popular and activist audiences beyond the spatial and imagined category of public, which isn't always a productive site of interaction. Take West and Dyson, for example. The more public they are, the less intellectual they become (if we conceptualize "intellectual" as a progressive and contestatory phenomenon).

I am interested in the vocabulary of engagement and intervention when speaking of scholars stepping outside the ivory tower. The distinction between something academic and nonacademic is not as trenchant as we might suppose. In the humanities especially, undertaking research is a fundamentally public process, by which I mean it is a process that inevitably entails an encounter with social systems and societies. I reject, as do many others these days, the idea that scholars must be disinterested observers of social systems and societies (the private option) and never participants in them (the public option). Scholars affect the same communities they purport to study from a distance. These effects need not be automatically negative. In fact, the intellectual has nothing stopping him or her from engaging communities in ways that might be mutually beneficial. Communal intervention, of a type that is consensual and constructive, represents a shift away from an ambiguous notion of the public intellectual. One often achieves the status of a "public intellectual," above and beyond untitled public positions, by cultivating a pundit brand, which results not in the production of scholarship but in what Houston Baker Jr. calls "pamphlet literature."[34]

An intervention needs to occur in order to challenge Israel's status as an essential component of multicultural conviviality, a status West and Dyson have played a considerable role in maintaining. Their role in its maintenance cannot be separated from their prominence as public intellectuals, though I again point to their rare intervention, despite their public eminence, in the reorganization of unjust social and economic structures. Perhaps their lack of radical intervention has enabled their public eminence. In any case, their complicity in the conflation of Israel and Jewish culture, or in the conflation of recognizing Israel as a recognition of Jewish culture, is questionable ethically and careless intellectually. For West and Dyson, accepting the basic premise of Zionism is a source of multicultural decorum. It should be a source of scrutiny and skepticism instead.

In a broader sense, we need to complicate the perception that diversity and multiculturalism are intuitively valuable phenomena. Even if we accept that they are valuable as concepts, their practice is problematic because it is manifestly exclusionary. It is impossible to raise a notion of multicultural celebration that doesn't preclude myriad groups from accessing the realm of culture. Were such a feat possible, I still would have misgivings about seeking transethnic understanding through the current practices of diversity and multiculturalism. My primary misgiving is that diversity and multiculturalism have become corporatized—and indeed have a corporate origin—leading to an institutionalization of the concepts that disallows them to threaten the institutions in which the problems of racism and iniquity are housed. Another misgiving is that diversity and multiculturalism can be used as marketing strategies more easily than they can evoke useful discourses of contestation. Multiculturalism is a propitious element of West and Dyson's market niche, not an object of their critical attention. I base this assessment on the fact that their pundit brands enable them to enter spaces in which diversity and multiculturalism are valued; they are not called to do the sort of analytical work in which the value of diversity and multiculturalism as modes of engagement are questioned.

The exclusions that accompany these concepts are especially harmful vis-à-vis Arabs and Muslims, who do not often make their way into the celebratory spaces of liberal tolerance. That they do not often enter into these spaces is a matter of design and not merely a regrettable coincidence. Liberal Zionists have forced themselves into spaces of multiculturalism so effectively that the celebration of Israel as a feature of Jewish identity is de rigueur, while dialogue with Arabs, many of them vocally anti-Zionist, is ignored if not discouraged. One should check the events in one's local community to get a sense of how infrequently Arabs are invited to attend celebrations of diversity, or even how rarely they are asked to speak about Arab cultures and politics, a job generally reserved for white Orientalists or former Israeli soldiers. Arabs are institutionally excluded from the normative conceptions of American diversity. For example, a profile by Ta Nehisi Coates in

The Nation of new NAACP president Benjamin Jealous recounts
the following story:

> When Jealous was 18, he was stopped on Columbia's cam-
> pus by an FBI officer who mistook him for an Iraqi stu-
> dent. (Jealous had spent the previous week protesting the
> Gulf War.)
> "I went off on him about why I looked the way
> I looked," says Jealous, referring to his ancestry. "That
> was the moment that I really realized I had ownership in
> this country. And for him to suggest that I didn't belong
> here. . . . I went off."[35]

Jealous's opposition to the Gulf War and his refusal to allow
appearance to dictate belonging are both admirable, but there are a
few implicit problems with the scene Coates describes. The notion
of belonging through which Coates frames Jealous's story is tacitly
exclusionary, but in a different way than the FBI officer's exclusionary attitude. To the FBI officer, being Arab justifies implicit suspicion. To Jealous (as he is presented by Coates), being Arab denotes
a lack of belonging that to him, of mixed white and black background, is offensive. Jealous didn't go off on the FBI officer because
of the officer's anti-Arab racism; he went off on him because his
blackness wasn't recognized as contradistinctive of foreignness.

Other conceptions of multicultural belonging demand inclusions
of ethnonationalism. Public intellectuals such as West and Dyson
are asked to latently reaffirm these exclusions by participating in
dialogues with liberal Zionists who openly demand affirmation of
Israel's right to exist as a Jewish state (i.e., to be juridically racist). West and Dyson concede such an affirmation without demanding anything in return but a microphone and an audience. (West's
troublesome performance in *Jews and Blacks* repeatedly illustrates
his timidity when it comes to Zionism's aggressiveness.) Instead of
asking why no regular dialogue with Arabs and Muslims, which is
a useful question, I would rather ask why West and Dyson regularly allow affirmations of Israel to be compulsory to an acceptable
multicultural agenda. The silence in liberal American discourses
around Palestinian suffering is nearly absolute. West and Dyson
are in a position to make substantial portions of the American

people aware of that suffering, which is the terrible irony of the whole enterprise: they have achieved their exalted position because of a certain agreeableness where renunciation is ethically requisite. I raise this rigid point not as an injunctive judgment but because all intellectuals should stand firm on the principle that colonization is never acceptable.

The Christian traditions to which West and Dyson belong as members of the black clergy uphold forms of justice that are commensurate with opposition to Zionism. The forms of liberation theology that arise from these traditions aren't always easily put into transit. They contain liberal ideas of acceptance and reconciliation that create tension between their universal humanism and the realities of injustice that Israel's very presence cultivates. The tension exists because Israel's supporters have adamantly maintained that their support of the state accords with or is essential to universal humanism. We need to think about ways to critically examine these claims, which generally don't hold up to ethical scrutiny. It might also be useful to contemplate Palestine beyond the intellectual traditions of American multiculturalism and the complexities of race relations in the United States. There is a specific archetype of colonization that attends Israel's existence and its current practices that is best analyzed in the framework of the United States as an expansionist power rather than as a multiethnic agglomeration. And there is a standard of courage around Palestine that West and Dyson have yet to exhibit: if Zionists are going to conceal Israel's ethnic cleansing behind quaint discourses of multicultural decorum, then we must confront that decorum with proud indecency.

4   Sexuality, Violence, and Modernity in Israel

The Paradise of Not Being Arab

> Art is magic delivered from the lie of being truth.
>
> —THEODOR ADORNO, *MINIMA MORALIA*

Much of Zionism's humanistic discourse relies on affirmation through negation: Iran is irresponsibly nuclear (implying that Israel deserves its nuclear weapons even though it still hasn't confessed to having them), Arabs and Muslims are irrationally violent (implying that Israel is peaceable or uses violence judiciously), Arab states are backward and Third World (implying that Israel is cosmopolitan and European). The latest Zionist intervention into the culture wars is especially clever and equally disingenuous: the Arabs are incurably homophobic (implying that Israel is modern and open-minded if we allegorize queers as canaries and civic attitudes as coal mines). In 2009 StandWithUs, an emergent Zionist organization, sponsored a campaign claiming that Israel is a gay paradise and that gay Arabs and Muslims, persecuted in their own societies, find sanctuary in an open-minded Israel. But are these claims true? More important, what do the discourses underlying them suggest about the delusions of Zionism and the profound desire of its advocates to position Israel in supposedly modernistic spaces?

In undertaking analysis of these questions, I draw on and build from the work of Jasbir Puar, whose *Terrorist Assemblages* explores the interconnection of sexuality and the violence of the nation-state.[1] Puar's theoretical inquiry is superb but enters into intellectual terrain too ambitious for this project. However, I apply some of her theoretical innovations to the newfangled propaganda initiatives around homosexuality and Israeli tolerance. There are fruitful connections to be made between the relationship of feminism with colonization and the identification of purported homophobia as a marker of premodernity. Lots of work has assessed the entanglement of certain forms of Western feminism in militaristic imperialism.[2] This entanglement involves various political axes and ethical commitments. Of primary importance here is the ability of a humanistic idea such as feminism to be put into the service of war or oppression. That ability connects it to what Puar calls homonational narratives, which refer loosely to the integration of national consciousness, including patriotism, and colonialist narratives of moral superiority (in this case, superiority in the form of advanced sexual consciousness). While the terms of imperialist discourses of feminism and homonationalism differ, dramatically in some cases, the use of such discourses as an indicator of proper modernity relies on the same ethical assumptions. The phenomenon is both fascinating and troublesome, and I highlight its rhetorical characteristics and political uses in the following.

Paradise to Gay Palestinians?

Israel, according to some activists and advocacy organizations, is unusually gay friendly given its location in the Middle East, a place of intractable homophobia. An advertisement in the 2009 campaign of StandWithUs asks, "Why does Israel look like paradise to gay Palestinians?" The advertisement, which ran in numerous publications, displays the slogan, "Israel respects life." This slogan is nonspecific, but it needn't specify anything to get its point across. By proclaiming that Israel is a paradise—something of a propitious savior of the culturally unfortunate—for Palestinians suffering the brutality of their own history, StandWithUs uses a homonational claim as a synecdoche of Israeli civility in general. Two notable ironies emerge: (1) Israel is absolved of its colonial and military policies, which entail an unmistakable disrespect for Palestinian lives. (2) Israel is contextualized by the Middle East but it ceases to be located there; StandWithUs positions it in a community of modern nations exclusive of Arab and Muslim states and allusive of a cultured European orientation. In reference to the second point,

StandWithUs does not conceptualize Israel in spatial terms; it does so through allusion to imagined geopolitical cohorts in Europe, whose acceptance of homosexuals separates the region from the Muslim backwaters of Asia and Africa. Another advertisement sponsored by StandWithUs reinforces this civilizational binary through heavy-handed suggestion. The obvious image here is a noose, which drops into the ad almost serendipitously despite its spookiness, from an unseen hangman or apparatus. The main point of the noose is conspicuous: being gay in Palestine is the equivalent of a death sentence. It suggests premodern forms of punishment, in keeping with the sort of irrationality that attends Arab homophobia. The noose is not only threatening; it is also arbitrary, stuck in a dark age whence the attitudes underlying it emerge. The facts StandWithUs cites in both ads are debatable, something I examine more closely later. At this point, we can note that the "facts" are part of the spectacle, crudely rendered testaments to the irredeemable horror of Palestinian barbarity.

StandWithUs is not a lone crusader. Other groups have taken up the cause of homonationalism. The Israel Project, an ardently Zionist outfit, released a report in 2008 extolling Israel's progressive values, as exemplified by its commitment to gay rights. The point of the report is not to congratulate Israel, however. It is to demonize the Palestinians: "There are several explanations about how Israel has come to embrace its gay and lesbian community. One is that the family as an institution is central to Israeli Jewish society. Therefore, parents would rather accept their lesbian, gay, bisexual and transgender (LGBT) children than let homophobia destroy family unity."[3] This analysis implies that Palestinians are neither family oriented nor tolerant; they are willing to sacrifice their own children to their irrational beliefs, or they are so irrational as to be unable to make such a choice. Even in its exaltation of Israeli open-mindedness, the Israel Project betrays its own implicit homophobia: homosexuality is not embraced by Israeli Jews; it is merely tolerated in the interest of family unity. It is not something Israeli Jews would ever accept; it simply presents a difficult obstacle that they are reluctantly willing to overlook. If Israel is attempting to shore up its image based on this narrative, then perhaps it would be best for the state to lend the Israel Project to Hamas.

The Israel Project's commitments are better revealed later in the report:

> Israel is in many ways a Western society and therefore has a more liberal perspective than its Middle East neighbors on a variety of issues, including sexual orientation and sexuality. Finally, Israel, as a democratic and mostly secular society, has been a model for promoting the rights of all of its citizens, regardless of gender, religion or race.[4]

The discourses in this passage are dense with connotation. I examine the connotations in a moment. First, it is necessary to point out that nearly everything in the passage is factually untrue. Israel requires all of its citizens, including non-Jews, to swear a loyalty oath to Israel as a Jewish state; it has banished Knesset member Azmi Bishara and otherwise marginalized dozens of other elected Arab politicians; it is currently removing Arabic from road signs and government buildings; it regularly harasses and beats Palestinian Israelis at checkpoints; and it destroys Bedouin homes and seizes their land, which then becomes state owned and reserved for the exclusive use of Jews. According to the Mossawa Center's 2009 report, forty-two Palestinian citizens of Israel have been killed by police violence since October 2007; seventeen Palestinian Israelis were subject to police brutality in 2008 alone. Jewish Israelis undertook seventy attacks on their Palestinian compatriots. Fifteen incidents of public service discrimination were reported, along with twenty-nine cases of racial incitement. Twelve bills that can be described as brazenly discriminatory were debated in the Knesset.[5] Even Ehud Olmert, former prime minister of Israel, has acknowledged that "there is no doubt that for many years there has been discrimination against the Arab population that stemmed from various reasons."[6]

The connotations of the passage are more disturbing than its assertions because the assertions are simple to debunk. The connotations require analysis to highlight a tacit perniciousness that belies the Israel Project's pretense of compassion. The idea of Israel as a Western society that eschews the Third World backwardness of its Arab neighbors is profoundly colonialist and duplicitous in its rhetorical objective, which is to rationalize through humanistic adornment Israel's usurpation of Palestinian land, resources, and peoplehood. It recapitulates the venerable notion of civilizational superiority as an ipso facto rationale for violence and militarism. StandWithUs also suggests that only democracies and secular polities can achieve the status of sexually evolved. However, in reality it is in many supposedly premodern indigenous communities that nontraditional sexualities have long been accepted. In the industrialized West, on the other hand, the underlying structure of nation-states is deeply heteronormative in addition to being sexist, racist, and religiously mediated. The construction of these secular states has been a conduit of homophobia, not its saboteur. As we see later, this reality is especially the case with Israel.

The campaign to portray Israel as open-minded is not merely a pretext to colonize Palestinians; it informs the geopolitical context of Iran. Though groups like StandWithUs and the Israel Project are aligned with the Israeli state ideologically, in this case the groups and the state appear to be working on the agitprop of Israel's gay-friendliness in concert. In 2009 *Ha'aretz* reported that Israel's Foreign Ministry commenced oversight of a PR campaign to highlight Israel's modernity, with emphasis on its treatment of gay citizens. An anonymous senior political source explained the Foreign Ministry's reasoning: "We have to lay the foundation in the world, and particularly in Europe, in order to be able to take harsher steps against Iran, especially in the economic sector."[7] The multimillion-dollar PR campaign juxtaposes open-mindedness and civility with military belligerence. The only contradiction here is in the realm of logic, not of politics. The United States has long inscribed definitions of civility in the framework of military action, as in Iraq, Afghanistan, Kosovo, Panama, and Grenada. In fact, one of the hallmarks of civility and modernity as they have been constructed by their patrons is an eagerness to use violence to teach the uncivilized a severe lesson.

Amal Amireh points out that the Foreign Ministry's campaign "is bad news for homosexuals in Iran and for those who care about them."[8] She succinctly identifies why these humanistic arguments for military intervention are problematic. They are not only geopolitically bad ideas and morally dubious but also completely ineffectual if we accept the conceit that they are actually intended to aid victims of sexism and homophobia. It is difficult to imagine anybody who truly cares about women or homosexuals wanting their countries bombed, destabilized, or occupied militarily—these phenomena do not solve the original problems of sexism and homophobia; they add even more serious burdens to them and endanger more people than the original problems on their own ever could. Moreover, military intervention almost always amplifies the social problems it proclaims it opposes. In July 2009, for instance, two gay Iraqi refugees claimed that U.S. soldiers displayed signs reading "Fuck Off Fags" and targeted gay Iraqis for execution (claims denied by the American military).[9] Not in question is that, since the 2003 American invasion of Iraq, violence against gay Iraqis has increased substantially.[10] There is no good reason to believe that economic sanctions or military action against Iran will in any way improve the lives of gay Iranians. All evidence points to the contrary, that these actions would result in increased persecution in addition to the needless death of Iranian civilians of all backgrounds.

Much of the problem is with particular discursive traditions in the West. The nation-state is an anointed site of ethnic liberation, even though it is usually within the strictures of nation-states that heteronormativity attains juridical and social validation. Because of the long tradition of couching colonial politics in the language of agonized benevolence, many activists in the West turn to military intervention as a natural solution to humanitarian crises elsewhere.[11] The racism that arises from colonization and militarism can influence the liberal discourses of advocacy, which often focus on desultory matters like tolerance and coexistence rather than on modes of structural inequality or prejudice. In the case of homonationalism, resistance to repressive state policies can easily lead to support of a different set of repressive state policies. For instance, an imagined affinity by Western gay rights activists with gay people in the Arab World, widely believed to be incurably homophobic, can expose implicit prejudices and power disparities.

In one case, *The Advocate* commentator James Kirchick lambastes lesbian Palestinian Rauda Morcos for not being friendly enough to Israel: "She is unable to appreciate the advantages of Israel's liberal society," he complains.[12] Kirchick asserts that "it is the freedom that Israel grants not just to gays but to all of its minority citizens—especially Arab Muslims and Christians—that allows Morcos to so heedlessly denigrate the free society that she inhabits."[13] Ultimately, "gays around the world should be hoping that a future Palestinian state looks more like Israel, and not the other way around."[14] The factual inaccuracies of Kirchick's analysis should by now be clear. The most noteworthy feature of his article is its hypocrisy. Beyond the specter of a white male lecturing a Palestinian woman about how she ought to perceive her own country, Kirchick appears to believe that Palestine belongs not to the Palestinians but to the international gay community. It is clear that when he extols the advantages of "Israel's liberal society," he has in mind advantages for Westerners—specifically, Western Zionists or gay tourists—and thinks nothing of the Palestinians, the people indigenous to the area in the first place. Kirchick illustrates that, in the gay-is-modern-thus-modern-is-Israel syllogism, gay rights will always supersede the civil and human rights of Palestinians, no matter what their gender identity or sexual orientation. His hypocrisy arises from the fact that in lambasting Palestinians for not being gay friendly enough—a position he developed without ever having spent time in Palestinian society and not reading or speaking Arabic—he forwards an ethical perspective in which gay rights must override all ethnic and national considerations. It is clear that he is much more committed to Israel's image than he is to the well-being of gay people. Kirchick shares this perspective with Israel's Foreign Ministry, StandWithUs, and the Israel Project. Perhaps the saddest or funniest part of the argument about gay Palestinians finding sanctuary in Israel is that Palestinians aren't allowed to emigrate there, no matter what their sexuality. Entrance to Israel is reserved solely for Jews. Even if gay Palestinians wanted to escape to Israel, the very best they could hope for is harsh rejection.

These problems are all on display in the iPRiDE program in Tel Aviv sponsored by StandWithUs. The program is supposed to be about "Israel's culture in a GLBT scope," but in reality it is a celebration of Zionist mythology.[15] The LGBT issues are merely a pretext to assert Jewish belonging in the Holy Land and to supplement Israel's rationalization of ethnic cleansing by underscoring its commitment to modernity. One panel is titled "100th Anniversary to [sic] Tel-Aviv: From a Desert of Ignorance to an Oasis of Sexual Freedom." Another is "Don't Ask Don't Tell? Not in Israel! Israeli Establishments from a Gay Perspective." The panel explores being

openly gay in the Israeli occupation forces (IOF). The event intimates that gay people in Israel cannot speak against colonization but they are welcome to participate in it. Their equal rights,
in other words, come at the cost of loyalty to the state of Israel.
The state in question is working hard to erase the physical and
cultural presence of Palestinians. That much is clear in the panel
on Tel Aviv, which reproduces the venerable image of Palestine as
an empty wasteland that industrious Jews selflessly redeemed. The
conferral of desert imagery and its connotation of backwardness to
Arabs contrast sharply with the modern oasis the Israelis reserve
for themselves, an oasis exemplified by the supposed presence of
sexual freedom.

Stand with Whom?

Who is this organization, StandWithUs, that seems to have
appeared out of nowhere? It was founded in 2001 and undertakes
a range of activities on behalf of Israel, including distribution of
posters and leaflets, delegitimization of antioccupation activists,
campus agitprop, pressure on media, and vocal support of all
Israeli policies. StandWithUs is remarkably active. Its guidebook
Israel 101, intended for use by college students, is a glossy and
cheerful recapitulation of hard-line Zionist propaganda. Arab and
Muslim activists on campus will be familiar with its work even if
they are not specifically familiar with the organization. "Us" represents adamant Zionists, with whom everybody with a proper consciousness should stand.

   If any narrative favorable to Palestinians or critical of Israel,
even moderately, emerges in corporate media or on college campuses, StandWithUs answers the challenge, always using the
heavy-handed tactics of a zealous political operative. When Israel
boycotted the 2009 UN Durban Review Conference because of the
criticism it stood to face, StandWithUs released a series of posters
condemning the UN. The move itself isn't especially notable, as it
is what one would expect from an organization whose mission is
to support Israel. The viciousness of the posters is notable, however. For a mainstream organization, StandWithUs gets away with
an uncommon malevolence. One of the posters shows Palestinians
in white sheets—for American viewers undertones of the KKK are

inevitable—with green headbands marked with "Muslim" writing, explosive belts around their chests. Amid the men is a small child, also wearing faux explosives, one of the adults lovingly patting his head, a jarring correlation of violence and affection. Admonishing the UN for not condemning Palestinian "child abuse," the poster endeavors to achieve maximum shock value by invoking every trope of Palestinian subhumanity.[16] As with some initiatives on the political right, StandWithUs appropriates the same language of human rights its adversaries use to criticize Israel.

Another poster employs the same motif. Devoid of images, it reads "Defending Israel Against Terrorism is a Human Right! Support Israel!"[17] The idea of Israel as a human rights sanctuary contravenes both legal and political definitions of the term, but the poster is effective not because of truth—which in any case is very difficult to locate in slogans—but because of its suggestiveness. By framing the words "Against Terrorism" with a red border, the image evokes bloodshed and draws spectators to the all-important word "Terrorism," which has a coterminous relationship with Palestinians in Zionist ideologies. The image creates numerous binaries useful to the message StandWithUs wants to impart: Israel, good/Palestinians, bad; Israel, victim/Palestinians, aggressors; Israel, humanist/Palestinians, terrorists; Israel, defensive/Palestinians, belligerent; Israel, human rights champion/Palestinians, human rights violators; Israel, worthy of support/Palestinians, worthy of disdain. Framed by two horizontal blue bars meant to represent Israel's flag, the poster highlights all the key concepts of hard-line Zionist propaganda. It offers Zionist activists a simple, concise way to disseminate their talking points through visual and textual significations. Reducing the Israel-Palestine conflict to a set of talking points limited to Jewish victimization and innate Palestinian violence is the modus operandi of all Zionist organizations.

Without question, the most evocative of the posters of StandWthUs is the one produced amid Israel's 2008–2009 destruction of the Gaza Strip. Its text reads "Stop The Use Of Human Shields In Gaza."[18] Above the text is a picture of dancing skeletons, big and small, reminiscent of the Grateful Dead's dancing bears. The big skeletons raise tilted Qassam rockets, presumably aimed at Israel. The small ones are wearing bibs—in case viewers aren't quite sure that they are child skeletons—emblazoned with "human shield" in red lettering, matching the tips of the Qassams. As with the poster depicting Hamas militants, the trope of the child terrorist is central. Even though the Palestinian child is a menace, he is also innocent, ushered unwittingly into violence by his parents and superiors. He can be saved, but not if he remains Palestinian; it is the savage culture he is in that ensures his degeneracy. His elders care more about killing Jews than raising him to be a good person. This is demonstrated by his enlistment to be a human shield at so young an age. It is not his fault, but he is still culpable. His life, like that of all Palestinians, is hopeless. It would have been much better for him had he been born a Jew.

I have already illustrated that the charge that Palestinians use human shields is indemonstrable, that it is Israel that has been implicated repeatedly in the practice, including the use of children. No credible evidence has been found that Palestinians abuse or endanger their children in the way zealots and propaganda operatives claim. Such claims rely in no small part on racist notions that Palestinians value life less than Jews do. In reality, the greatest threat to Palestinian children is the Israeli military, which has killed nearly 1,500 Palestinian children since late 2000.[19] This number is considerably greater than the Palestinian children killed by abuse, neglect, and faulty hand grenades combined. The point of agitprop is not accuracy but the advancement of extant perceptions favorable to the ideology of the sponsoring organization. The idea that Palestinians do not value life and that Jews are the victims of irrational Arab hatred has a deep foundation in the United States, mainly through Zionist ideologues and uncritical corporate media. Keeping emphasis on these perceptions is of primary import to StandWithUs. If we discuss these perceptions, then we won't be discussing the facts of Israel's behavior, which can only make the state look mendacious.

Given the facts of Israel's treatment of Palestinians, it is reasonable to conceptualize the promotional campaigns of StandWithUs as racist, for they lock Palestinians into a simulation that belies the actuality of their existence. The simulated existence into which Palestinians are locked treats them as incurably hostile and always menacing, given to outbursts of violence and indifferent to the well-being of their own children. StandWithUs and its peers are asking us to support gay people by becoming racists. We are thus to trade in antiracist and anticolonialist consciousness for a gay rights mythology that merely buttresses the infelicities of nationalism. There are better ways to challenge homophobia. There are more humane ways to think about suffering and power. Those using homosexuality as a rhetorical bludgeon represent propaganda outfits no decent person would ever think about standing with.

Gay-Friendly Israel?

Thus far I have not challenged the central assumption of the initiatives under critique, that Israel is a gay paradise, especially compared to Arab states, which subscribe to a medieval Islam that renders them terminally homophobic. Is Israel as gay friendly as Zionist activists assert? The evidence illustrates that it is not—and it is certainly not gay friendly enough to justify the paeans to its modernity proffered by James Kirchick, StandWithUs, Israel's Foreign Ministry, and others.

One might measure gay-friendliness in various ways. StandWithUs and others do it based on Israeli laws that provide equal protection for gays and allow them to serve openly in the military (which is another way of saying that gays are not allowed to escape compulsory military service). However, in Israel gays are not allowed to marry; the institution of marriage for Jews falls under the authority of Israel's Chief Rabbinate, which is unlikely to overturn the ban anytime soon. It is a shortsighted view of gay rights to judge them based primarily on juridical benchmarks, which often forbid access to civil rights or supplement unjust forms of state power, such as imperialism or invasive surveillance, both serious problems in Israel. Other ways of measuring gay-friendliness include freedom of movement and access to a cross-range of public and private spaces, the safety of those presumed to be gay or transgendered, and the representation of LGBT people by politicians and in popular culture. These measurements, along with the limited rights of LGBT people, illustrate that the portrayal of Israel as a gay paradise is more propaganda than substance. While Israel has a more progressive legal apparatus around homosexuality than the United States, it is no panacea and certainly not progressive enough for Zionists to uphold it as a model of justice. In conjunction with Israel's rampant human rights abuses against Palestinians,

Lebanese, and its ethnic minority citizens, Israel's supposed affection for LGBT people is an unusually ironic mythology in a country replete with myth and irony.

While StandWithUs and others extol Israel's hosting of a gay pride parade, they fail to mention that a significant segment of Israeli society opposed the parade. Shas Party interior minister Eli Yishai and the country's chief rabbis sent a letter to prime minister Benjamin Netanyahu urging him to cancel the parade. The letter warned, "Even in a constitutional democracy sensitive. to the freedom of expression, there is no right to allow the consumption of abominations."[20] In 2008 parliamentarian Shlomo Benizri blamed earthquakes on homosexuality: "I suggest that the Knesset inquire into how it can prevent sodomy and thus save us a lot of earthquakes."[21] Although this method of earthquake prevention isn't yet scientifically proved, it does cohere with the utterly premodern recommendations for averting natural disasters offered by some religious leaders in the United States. In 2007 Rabbi Einat Ramon of Jerusalem's Schechter Rabbinical Seminary, a devoted feminist, upheld the exclusion of homosexuals despite the fact that the world Conservative movement chose to permit their ordination; Ramon pointed to the "historic centrality of heterosexual unions to Judaism."[22]

StandWithUs and others might point to the fact that this homophobia arises from religious quarters. This observation is correct, but it makes little difference for two reasons: (1) the populations represented by these homophobic leaders are a substantial demographic in Israel, and (2) Israel is itself a state premised exclusively on religious identity. It is untenable to separate the rabbinical forms of Judaism from secular Jewish cultures when it comes to citizenship and belonging; it is the non-Jews for whom this distinction might be notable. Moreover, it is the devoutly religious of all three primary monotheistic faiths most vocal in condemnation of homosexuality. StandWithUs cannot cite Islamic opposition to homosexuality but ignore the identical forms of Judaic opposition within Israel, at its highest levels of governance and power. It is also worth pointing out that religious communities tend to be most vocal in their condemnation, but it proves nothing about actual levels of homophobia; it proves only levels of vocality. If there weren't widespread secular homophobia in both the United States and

Israel, the equal rights for which LGBT people have been agitating would have long ago been ratified. In any case, there is one way in particular in which ostensibly secular groups like StandWithUs share an important outlook with religious organizations: both use homosexuality as a way to foreground anti-Arab politics. Author and rabbi Pinchas Winston asks, "Why does this war [Israel's 2006 invasion of Lebanon] break out this week, all of a sudden with little warning? Because this is the exact week the Jewish people are trying to decide whether the gay pride parade should take place in Jerusalem or Tel Aviv."[23] Winston might be considered both secular and religious. Either way, he expresses a common sentiment. In Israel, everything from Arab terrorism to Hizbullah's growing power is attributed to the presence of homosexuals in the Holy Land. StandWithUs and its peers make an identical argument in the inverse: Arabs are terrorists because they refuse to accommodate homosexuals. In both arguments, moral and intellectual stupidity presupposes a view of Arabs and Muslims that is viciously racist and exploitative, as it relies on a lack of Arab and Muslim agency to appropriate the arguments for the sake of their own disenfranchisement.

Palestinians inside Israel and in the Occupied Territories exist continuously under the threat of violence. They share this burden with LGBT people, Jewish or otherwise. In the summer of 2009, a gunman killed three people and wounded at least ten others, mostly teenagers, at a gay community center in Tel Aviv, an act that was met with widespread complaints of police inaction.[24] In 2005 a man wielding a knife stabbed three participants in Jerusalem's gay pride parade before being subdued by police. Several bombs containing homophobic notes have been defused; others presumed to have been motivated by homophobia have exploded. The übermacho New Jew created by early Zionists has held sway, as many in Israel still associate homosexuality with weakness and femininity, the latter association representing a conflation of sexist attitudes with homophobia. The presence of evangelical Christians in Israel also complicates the pursuit of gay rights. Zionist Christians from the United States are adamantly antigay and wield considerable influence in Israeli politics and society. They have lobbied government and religious leaders on behalf of their conservative Jewish allies, going so far as to suggest that the open presence of gays will lead to greater terrorism against Jews because the stereotype of the ugly American will have been exported to Israel.[25]

Israel's gay rights activists, like the rest of Israel's Jewish community, cannot extricate themselves from the ubiquity of Arabs. Nearly every discourse meant to identify a crucial element of Israel's national identity is deployed in an oppositional rather than affirmational fashion—that is to say, in opposition to what Israeli Jews imagine Arabs not to be rather than a clear sense of what they can affirm about themselves. If the Arabs are indelibly homophobic, then Israelis must be the chic and sophisticated moderns immortalized in programs like *Sex and the City*. The question of sexuality in the Arab World isn't so simple, though. While it is easy to conceptualize the Arab and Muslim worlds as intolerant of LGBT people, in keeping with their rabid predilections in general, their cultural and political realities, as in all other places on earth, are significantly more nuanced and complicated.

Zionist claims of Arab and Muslim homophobia cannot be separated from the benefits they derive from bastardizing Arabs and Muslims, the abject ignorance most of them have about the region, and a chronic set of assumptions that Arabs and Muslims are incapable of entering into modernity, of which gay-friendliness is a benchmark. It might be novel or naïve to expect professional propagandists to make comments based on evidence, but the mythology of unbending Arab homophobia has lately become so widespread that it warrants a critical response even though numerous studies rigorously belie that mythology. One of the early analyses of sexuality in the Arab World, Edward Said's *Orientalism*, illustrates that the images of Arab sexual appetites for women, men, and children are indivisible from perceptions of their sexual practices.[26] Indeed, it is only recently that the image of Arabs as vicious homophobes has become customary in Western colonialist discourses; such images are necessary to the construal of Arabs and Muslims as premodern. Any portrayal of a people's sexual proclivities will involve simulation, especially peoples as diverse as Arabs and Muslims, who, like all other people, abide by no homogeneous norms.

Because many Zionists treat *Orientalism* as if it were an exercise in fanaticism, it is not surprising that Said's analysis of Eastern sexualities has widely been ignored or misinterpreted. Said points out that we cannot rightly distinguish shifts in representation from the evolution of organic cultures and practices. Nevertheless, there is no good excuse for those interested in Arab and Muslim sexualities not to peruse the rigorous scholarship that has been produced about multivalent sexual cultures and practices in Arab and Muslim societies. Much of the representation of Arab and Muslim sexual practice is actually the projection of Western travelers, uninformed anthropologists, and political operatives. Noting that "sex was always an important feature of Orientalist fantasy and scholarship,"[27] Joseph Massad explains that *"incitement to discourse* on sexual rights outside the United States and Western Europe necessitated that human rights organizations and advocates incorporate existing anthropological knowledge of the non-Western world."[28] The incitement to discourse Massad identifies is a way of conjoining perception and action; activists can employ discourse to incite certain political actions, in the case of Zionist activists the incitement to colonization of Palestine and an American or Israeli invasion of Iran.

Massad's argument that perceptions of sexuality in the Arab World are integrated with long-standing and contradictory forms of Orientalism is validated by ample scholarship. The collection *Islamicate Sexualities*, edited by Kathryn Babayan and Afsaneh Najmabadi, presents a complex view of sex and homosexuality and the representations of both in Muslim communities. Contradistinctive of the simplistic portrayals offered by StandWithUs, *Islamicate Sexualities* illuminates dynamic forms of sexual play and signification throughout Islamic Asia, including examination of the once-predominant view in Europe that homosexuality is rampant and accepted in the Arab World, to its detriment.[29] Khaled El-Rouayheb points out that, in writing a history of homosexuality, "one assumes that the concept 'homosexual,' like the concept 'woman,' is shared across historical periods, and that what varies and may be investigated historically is merely the changing cultural (popular, scientific, legal, etc.) attitude toward such people."[30] El-Rouayheb argues that "Arab-Islamic culture on the eve of modernity lacked the concept of 'homosexuality,' and that writings from the period do not evince the same attitude toward all aspects of what we might be inclined to call homosexuality today."[31] Even if El-Rouayheb's argument is debatable, his broader point is important: we cannot represent a people's cultural epochs without considering that people in the context of their own traditions and vocabularies.

The instabilities of tendentious representation are obvious vis-à-vis Arab and Muslim sexualities. Orientalists and others basically have transformed Arabs and Muslims from lascivious debauchees into puritanical autocrats. But there are more obvious and troubling ways that Arabs and Muslims have been sexualized in Western discourse and practice. It is a ruthless irony that those who project sexual simulacra onto Arabs and Muslims like to perform those perceptions on Arab and Muslim bodies. The discursive and visual sexualization of Arabs and Muslims is inseparable from their physical sexualization through modes of torture arising from coercive state power. It is well known by Palestinians that anytime one of them enters or exits Israel, regardless of nationality, he or she will likely undergo an anal or vaginal probe. These probes, as in the American prison system and in police stations around the world, aren't intended to be pragmatic. They are acts of psychological domineering and political assertion. The agents of these coercive actions are rehearsing their own depravity through fulfillment of their Orientalist notions of Arab and Muslim sexuality.

Such was the case in Abu Ghraib, whose horrors have been only partially revealed. The pictures that were revealed of the torture illustrate that Arab homosexuality was scripted. The Arab male body became a repository for an American gaze, whose presence constituted the bodies' positionalities in the first place. It appeared at first that the prisoners in Abu Ghraib were photographed in the most intimate of fashions, but a measured assessment reveals that there was nothing intimate about their closeness and nudity. The prisoners were forced into certain positions specifically so they could be dehumanized by being made to act out American fantasies of Arab sexual taboos. The fantastical Zionist conceptions of Arab and Muslim illiberalism and homophobia not only are inaccurate but also contradict Zionists' own Orientalist origins. They are likewise not even fanciful observations, but inventions of geopolitical need whose usefulness is rarely lost on Zionist ideologues. Even that supposed agent of crude postethnicity, Sacha Baron Cohen, has relied on the Zionist myths of Arab sexual repression and oppression. In his 2009 film, *Bruno*, Baron Cohen assumes the persona of a flamboyantly gay Austrian journalist named Bruno, whose quest for fame leads him to outrageous behavior. As satire, *Bruno* is a poor film. As social comment, it is more exploitative than insightful.[32] When Bruno visits the West Bank, the film subtly circulates a common justification for ethnic cleansing: Palestinian premodernity and its consequently violent intolerance.

Baron Cohen undertakes an ultradangerous, top-secret mission to interview a real, live Palestinian terrorist, an act of uncanny courage facilitated by an unnamed CIA contact. In an interview with David Letterman, "Baron Cohen explained that finding a 'terrorist' to interview for the movie took several months and some help from a CIA contact. He described the secular Martyrs Brigades, most of whom signed an amnesty deal with Israel in 2007, as 'the number one suicide bombers out there.'"[33] He also bragged to Letterman that "I thought I needed security. . . . It was in the West Bank. The guy picks this secret location. . . . The terrorist comes in with his bodyguard. I was pretty sure that my terrorist either did or did not have a gun on him."[34] Baron Cohen apparently risked life and limb, as Bruno might quip, in the interest of art and satire. This mysterious terrorist, however, is Ayman Abu Aita, a resident of Beit Sahour, the town that was nominated for a Nobel Peace Prize for its courageous nonviolent resistance. Abu Aita is a vocal advocate of nonviolence and a midlevel Fatah bureaucrat who has never been implicated in any crime, much less a crime as hideous as terrorism (Fatah is the late Yasser Arafat's political party). The secret location of their tryst was the popular Everest Hotel and Restaurant in nearby Beit Jala. The secret interview occurred in one of the hotel's rooms. The terrorist's bodyguard is Sami Awad, the executive director of Holy Land Trust, a community group devoted to civic engagement and a nonviolent approach to organizing. Awad's blog, *Never Give Up*, is headed by the slogan "Trust in the Power of Nonviolence to Heal the World."

I have some personal experience in this part of the West Bank. My mother's family and my father-in-law, in fact, are from Beit Jala and know the families of those Baron Cohen implicated as terrorists. Indeed, I've eaten at the Everest Restaurant and found the food to be delicious. The restaurant, like nearly everything in Beit Jala, offers wonderful views of the Jews-only settlement of Gilo, built on a plateau that once contained forested land. If Baron Cohen found travel in Beit Jala difficult, then surely it was not because of Palestinian terrorists but because of the walls and checkpoints surrounding the town so that the residents of Gilo can move freely without the inconvenience of seeing Palestinians. I've also had the opportunity to meet Sami Awad, a nonviolence activist who is a thin five feet eight and is impeccably polite and affable. I have a high opinion of Awad, but he would not be my first choice for a bodyguard. I would much rather employ for that sort of job one of the many armed Israeli soldiers who are trained to kill and lack Awad's revulsion for the uses of violence.

Baron Cohen's appearance on Letterman is instructive. He romanticizes the terrorist as a mysterious and exclusively Palestinian object. Despite his lame joke about the terrorist maybe or maybe not carrying a gun, it is revealing that Baron Cohen refers to him by using possessive language, "my terrorist." (Abu Aita wasn't sporting a gun, if that makes a difference.) Baron Cohen suddenly has ownership of Abu Aita's image and body, and through his flamboyant playacting as Bruno imagined that he would be able to exploit image and body for both financial and ideological profit. (Baron Cohen is well known as a devoted Zionist.) In order to make his point, he relied on the existence of certain assumptions about Muslims generally and Palestinians specifically:

- They are viciously homophobic; thus it will be of great comedic value to send in a conspicuously gay journalist to interview its most extreme element.
- Identifying a Palestinian terrorist will present little challenge because his primary audience is willing to accept any Arab male in such a role.
- In seeking out a terrorist, hypothetical or real, a Palestinian would make a safe and illustrious choice.
- Homosexuality, as presented in the peculiar fashion of Bruno, contrasts most distinctly with the strange rituals of Islamic intolerance. (Abu Aita is actually Christian, which makes no difference to Baron Cohen's methodology, though Abu Aita's religious background was identified by many commentators as if to proffer further proof that he couldn't possibly be a terrorist.)

The scene and its problematic context illuminate the usefulness to Zionists of the widespread presupposition that Arabs and Muslims are backward, a condition exemplified by rampant homophobia. This backwardness is easy to expose (and exploit) by playacting a form of sexual deviance apparently offensive to their antediluvian sensibilities. Baron Cohen's possessiveness is justified. Abu Aita is very much Baron Cohen's terrorist: Baron Cohen anticipated him and then unleashed him on those by whom he was already invented. Abu Aita's physical body merely enters into the fanciful spaces of modernity that define him even before we know who he is. Baron Cohen's movie is not merely racist but also substandard art. Any satire that does nothing more than recapitulate propaganda from StandWithUs and Israel's Foreign Ministry is doing not the work of a devoted satirist but the compliant job of an ideological warrior.

As I indicated earlier, Jasbir Puar takes up many of these issues in *Terrorist Assemblages*. Puar points out that

> Israeli queers can be legitimated by the Israeli state as well as by transnational queerdom through the quest for and right of sovereignty, while Palestinian queers are teleologically read through the lens of Islamic fundamentalism rather than the Palestinian struggle for self-determination and statehood, an interest in progressive queer politics, or even a liberal humanist exegesis of desire.[35]

Puar explores the larger framework of the inscription of queer tolerance into modernity. She argues that "during this historical juncture, there is a very specific production of terrorist bodies against properly queer subjects."[36] Puar portends the strategies of *Bruno* and various Zionist operatives with uncanny insight. These strategies rely specifically, almost exclusively, on the vocabularies of homonationalism, which Puar describes as a sort of "homosexual nationalism" wherein "some homosexual subjects are complicit with heterosexual nationalist formations rather than inherently or automatically excluded from or opposed to them."[37] In the case of recent initiatives to distinguish a modern Israel from a premodern Palestine through the exaltation of Israeli gay-friendliness, homosexual subjects are both complicit in and appropriated by the discourses of insatiable Zionist nationalism.

As Puar explains,

> Delineating Palestine as the site of queer oppression—oppression that is equated with the occupation of Palestine by Israel—effaces Israeli state persecution of queer Palestinians. Israeli state persecution of queer Israelis—because Israel is hardly exempt from homophobic violence toward its own citizens regardless of religious or ethnic background—is erased in this trickle-down model of sloganeering.[38]

Puar identifies the most crucial element of the problem of Zionist homonationalism. While it may seem clever or innocuously disingenuous for groups like StandWithUs to undertake homonational propaganda campaigns, ultimately there is nothing innocuous about them. Many lives are at stake in this particular conflict; in turn, the strategies of homonationalism are deeply violent. These strategies are deeply violent because they not only supplement ongoing forms of ethnonationalism and colonization but also buttress the homophobic violence they claim to oppose. It will be a wonderful occasion if one day Palestinian Arab and Israeli Jewish queer activists come together in equal community in order to contest the forces of homophobia. As long as StandWithUs and the Israeli Foreign Ministry are the guardians of modern consciousness, though, such an alliance will be impossible. Such is the case because their real goal is to create a Holy Land without Palestinians. Even if that terrible goal were not the case, the alliance could not happen, anyway, for just as a mid-century suburban country club wary of Jews, Israeli territory is a resolutely private space, genteel and well-heeled, in which the Palestinians are not allowed.

Integrating Justice, Excluding Violence

The contestation of homophobia is of seminal importance everywhere in the world. But like all oppressive discourses, it must be contested in conjunction with an integrated focus on all social and institutional phenomena that preclude comprehensive human wellness. It is from the same set of power dynamics that racism, sexism, homophobia, and their cognates emerge. To challenge homophobia by promoting war and colonization is immoral as well as strategically ineffectual, a reliable way to ensure that homophobia continuously reproduces itself. It is important for us to think about the ways that activist engagement can be co-opted, misplaced, or manipulated. Just as scholarship entails the task of nuance and thoroughness, activism needs to be outfitted with a thoughtful ethical context that looks beyond its immediate goals and pursues integrative models of justice. An integrative model of justice is first and foremost a commitment to ending one type of oppression without supplementing or actively fostering other types of oppression. When StandWithUs utilizes the language of equality for LGBT people it does not extend that language to include equality for Palestinians, Muslims, and other dark-skinned victims of Israeli racism. Indeed, as Puar points out, such an appeal to equality isn't even inclusive of all LGBT people, only of those belonging to or supportive of the Israeli state. A noteworthy feature of these strategies is how often they reference the open-mindedness of the IOF, which illuminates an inherent militarism and a romanticization of violence in the enterprise, resulting in an aggressive conflation of human rights language with colonization.

The use of ostensible LGBT open-mindedness to generate support for Israel in both abstract and economic frameworks is another unfortunate example of how the liberal discourses of inclusiveness and modernity do not always perform what they promise. The groups that invoke Israel's gay-friendliness as a means of consigning the Palestinians to immutable barbarity draw from the civilizational grandstanding that has always rendered modernity violent in practice and vocabulary. They participate in discourses of tolerance and coexistence that often are tacitly exclusive of those who don't fit the paradigm of the modern sophisticate. StandWithUs and others assume an implicit recognition of Islamic cruelty by the genteel targets of their campaign. Judging by the success of their campaign—a judgment based on how many commentators took up the same issue—that assumption was accurate.

Noa Meir, organizer of the 2009 iPRiDE program, puts it this way: "GLBT rights are part of human rights, and when you see Israel, you see a country that has come so far in this area. . . . When people see that Israel is so progressive on this issue, they realize that it can't just be on this issue, and realize this must apply to

Israel as a whole."[39] The origin of the forum is especially revealing: "'The idea was partly inspired by reactions to Operation Cast Lead,' group leader Meir recalled—specifically, an incident in San Francisco that saw a gay organization of 20-somethings 'identifying with the Palestinian cause and publicly calling to 'free the gays in Israel.'"[40] This example of responsible political activism, not the supposed mistreatment of gays in Palestine, inspired StandWithUs to undertake its campaign. StandWithUs has much more work to do in repairing Israel's image, however. A 2009 *Ha'aretz* survey found that 46 percent of Israelis consider homosexuals to be deviant.[41] If gay paradise refers to a nation wherein half the population considers LGBT people degenerate, then maybe it is true that, in the immortal words of Meat Loaf, heaven can wait.

5 The Heart of Darkness Redux, Again

Artists don't make objects. Artists make
mythologies.

—ANISH KAPOOR, INTERVIEW WITH JOHN TUSA

Since the advent of Western colonization, it has been remarkably difficult for white subjects in the metropole to access their deepest psychological sensibilities. All too frequently they need to enter into worlds so alien and exotic that they have no choice but to undertake agonizing introspection. Such was the fate of legendary figures like Marlowe, Dances with Wolves (Lieutenant Dunbar), and Albert Camus. Luckily for white subjects, colonization provided them a nearly limitless geography of mystique, peril, and strangeness. Usually these forays into foreign territory are voluntary, but sometimes they are forced. No matter their origin, they always have this in common: the use of a foreign setting as a backdrop for a psychodrama that endeavors to clarify the anxieties of power and violence. The natives of these mysterious lands are instrumental to the psychodramas, though they rarely appear in them as anything other than a vague backdrop to painful moral reckoning.

Nobody captured this phenomenon as dynamically and brilliantly as Joseph Conrad in *Heart of Darkness*, the novella that has inspired dozens, maybe hundreds, of imitators. The heart of darkness has become a psychological leitmotif of colonial self-expression. One of the most exciting works of criticism of the past century is Chinua Achebe's "An Image of Africa: Racism in Joseph Conrad's *Heart of Darkness*," a piece that still keenly describes a specific imperialist mentality. Achebe deconstructs "the desire—one might even say the need—in Western psychology to set Africa up as a foil to Europe, as a place of negations at once remote and vaguely familiar, in comparison with which Europe's own state of spiritual grace will be manifest."[1] Achebe points to the indispensability of Africa, as it has been invented out of Western gazes, in the consciousness of Western psychological self-fashioning. While Africa has been the primary site of these tortured explorations, Achebe's observation represents a paradigm that exists wherever colonization has occurred. There is no such thing as an artistic tradition in colonial societies autonomous of the consistent nagging of darkly nettlesome hearts.

Zionist art has repeatedly used this sort of trope. Much of the nonfiction by well-heeled novelists like Amos Oz and David Grossman conceptualizes the Jewish encounter with Palestinians as morally stupefying or emotionally debilitating. Much of the liberal commentary in Israel recycles the same motif. The heart of darkness is prominent in Zionist cinema, by which I mean filmmaking consciously trained on the historical or ideological dimensions of Zionism or Israel. Three recent films stand out: Ari Sandel's *West Bank Story*, Steven Spielberg's *Munich*, and Ari Folman's *Waltz with Bashir*. I pay special attention to their various modes of scrutiny and self-reflection. Although these are very different films aesthetically and dissimilar politically, they all endow themselves with the burden of intense psychoemotional soul-searching. All three are deeply worried about the declining status of Israel's soul. All three rely on anonymous Palestinians to frame their central moral questions. All three are didactic, in that they desire a type of soulful restoration that they conceptualize as an ethnic birthright.

The feature of most interest in this art is an earnest but truncated assessment of disparate power, which American and Israeli films often approach from the point of view of befuddled exemplars of the majority culture. Filmmakers outfit the majority culture with an innocent origin that has been corrupted by the encounter with a barbaric adversary. Even when filmmakers reference or problematize this formula, it usually emerges intact as a tacit motif. *Munich* reproduces the formula with little self-awareness; *Waltz with Bashir* appears to be aware of the formula without ultimately transcending it; *West Bank Story* isn't sophisticated enough to do more than evoke the mythologies that comprise the formula. All three films, in their different ways, suggest that Israel's soul was once anchored to a purer ideal that constant forays into the strange world of Arabs have compromised. All suggest that Israel repeatedly crosses the invisible but tangible boundary between modernity and premodernity, threatening to erode that boundary irreparably.

A Western *West Bank Story*

The film short *West Bank Story* was the darling of the 2005 Oscar season. The film's success isn't surprising. Not only does it contain lighthearted moments and a happy theme; it also proffers the simplistic dialogic prescriptions for peace adored by Hollywood's liberal elite and by most well-heeled critics. These are the same prescriptions favored by Cornel West, Michael Eric Dyson, and other scholars and commentators who theorize dialogue and coexistence as the precursors of rapprochement while ignoring or downplaying the importance of social justice and reparations. *West Bank Story* offers a feel-good tale of coexistence for those who hate the nettlesome burden of justice.

Running twenty-one minutes, *West Bank Story* is a pastiche of *West Side Story* and *Romeo and Juliet.* Directed by Ari Sandel and written by Kim Ray and Sandel, the story takes place in "the West Bank, Palestine" and presents the destruction and subsequent reconciliation of two competing restaurants, Hummus Hut and Kosher King ("the chosen restaurant"). The film is meant to be a satire of the Israel-Palestine conflict with a feel-good ending in the service of peace. Its satire is clunky and tepid, however, and its feelgood message vividly illuminates why peace has thus far been elusive. *West Bank Story* is didactic and subtly propagandistic, at times borderline racist. The film purports to illustrate both the silliness and resolvability of the Israel-Palestine conflict, but all of the burdens of violence in the film are Palestinian. The Israelis eschew violence and are never compelled to do anything but humor Palestinian idiosyncrasy in order to establish peace.

The first problem with *West Bank Story* is its location. Its identification of the West Bank's location as "Palestine" is accurate and, in the context of Zionist politics, progressive, but the rest of the story then becomes an exercise in the mystification of colonization. If the story takes place on the West Bank, then there is no need for a rapprochement between the Jews and Palestinians represented in the story, for the Jews would be settlers and occupation soldiers. The matter of Israel's military occupation of Palestinian land is scarcely mentioned in the film. Jewish settlement of the West Bank is omitted entirely. The soldiers are there only to protect Israel from suicide bombers; the Palestinians seem grateful to have them. Sandel and Ray are intent on reducing the conflict to the myths of irrational equivalence favored by many liberal Zionist intellectuals. Ahmed (Joey Naber), owner of the Hummus Hut, yells, "This land was meant for Arabs" at Ariel (A. J. Tannen), owner of the Kosher King, who responds, "This land was meant for Jews." The two characters, within a split screen, then begin arguing over the space each is allotted.

This scene might actually be funny if it had anything to do with the conflict it purports to satirize. The Palestinians do not use the sort of messianic discourse that makes claims of belonging based on theology or biology. If they proclaim that they have a right to Palestine, it is not because the land was "meant" for them but because they have always been there. They make ethical, legal, and political claims to land. In *West Bank Story* the land is deterritorialized and presented as an impersonal context for ethnic struggle. In fact, the land is central not only to the conflict but also to the spiritual and material articulations of Palestinian culture. The notion of abstract competing claims proffered by Sandel actually precludes the possibility of reconciliation by obscuring the central issues of the conflict, which are unfavorable to Israel. The reduction of the conflict to competing messianic claims benefits Israel because its messianic claims are the very basis of Zionism and because the reduction frees Israel from the responsibility to respect the many international laws it violates. The mode of tribal rivalry or irrational ethnic conflict favored by the many intellectuals and artists I have discussed in this book, then, is a convenient way to dissolve a fundamental colonizer-colonized binary and in turn shift moral responsibility for the Israel-Palestine conflict to both parties. This shift, it is worth noting, is not itself equitable. As in *West Bank Story*, the Palestinians are always depicted as the more violent party.

The most troublesome dimension of the film, though, has to do with its profound male colonial fantasy. One of the opening scenes occurs at a checkpoint where Ahmed's sister Fatima (Noureen DeWulf), donning a *hijab*, smiles affectionately at David (Ben Newmark), the soldier manning the checkpoint. David returns her affection. Sandel is setting up a Shakespearean love story between members of feuding communities. The problem is that the Israel-Palestine conflict looks nothing like the acrimony between the Montagues and Capulets, nor anything like the Hatfields and McCoys, the Grangerfords and Shepherdsons, Gore Vidal and Truman Capote, or any other feud that is synonymous with antipathy of a mysterious and mythologized origin. The antipathy of the Israel-Palestine conflict is a direct result of a century-long process of colonization. It isn't impossible that a Palestinian woman would fall in love with a soldier manning a checkpoint, the acutest symbol of Israeli oppressiveness, but such a motif exists squarely in the realm of a projected sexual desire nourished by the enormity of colonial power. It is the Palestinian woman who must be subsumed into the physical salacity of the Israeli male, best represented by the prowess of a soldier, in order for peace to occur. This relationship is symbolically important to the film's general point of view because Fatima is risking her family's honor. The Palestinians are not only backward in their tribal worldview but shamed by the possibility of reconciliation with Jews (in this case Jewish settlers).

Fatima embodies Palestinian society in other ways. Her head is covered at the checkpoint but exposed when she is working at the Hummus Hut as a cashier. Before she politely takes a customer's order she shoots a machine gun into the air while ululating. The customer then orders "death by chocolate suicide bomber for dessert." If viewers find it difficult to detect a bit of satiric levity in the scene, it is because there is none. Like the other scenes involving Arab characters, it resembles a Palestinian minstrelsy performance more than a provocative satire. I am very forgiving of ethnic stereotypes as they are deployed in comic settings, especially when these stereotypes allow us to consider issues of political import. In *West Bank Story*, nothing near political import arises, as the Palestinians act out their stupid violence toward befuddled Jews who respond in ridiculous but logical fashion. Sandel's bias toward liberal Zionist mythologies is continually evident in the film's thematic commonplaces and representational inconsistencies. This perspective should not be terribly surprising given that the film's production credits do not include a single Palestinian.

Two scenes, both comic, best illuminate the film's recapitulation of Zionist imperatives. In one, David and Ahmed argue with one another and exchange barbs of "terrorist" and "occupier." This binary, intended to reveal dogmatic perceptions, is ineffectual. Even in its position as instructive satire, it offers the wrong lesson. A more useful and accurate binary would be that of occupier-civilian, for it is the Palestinian civilian population that suffers the afflictions of Israel's military occupation. Moreover, when David deems Ahmed a terrorist he is insulting him through the use of an untrue stereotype, one that is arguably racist. When Ahmed deems David an occupier he is completely accurate. Yet it is Ahmed who initiates the destruction of the restaurants through stupidity and closed-mindedness. In the allegory of the dueling restaurants, it is the Palestinian who incites the violence that must be overcome. At the end of the film, when the Jewish and Palestinian characters begin working together amid the ruins of the two restaurants, David is totally absolved of his role as an occupier. He is instead welcomed to stay, a colonial fantasy perhaps on a par with the one that imagines native women swooning over foreign soldiers. If David is an occupier, he cannot be a friend. Sandel wants it both ways, however, which presupposes the film's main allegorical comment: that Israel can be an occupier and nevertheless deserve peace, that it can be ethnocentric and nevertheless accepted by those it excludes, that it can be unaccountable for its violence and nevertheless absolved by those who suffer that violence.

To that end, the choice to make David a soldier is curious and possibly foolish. Popular culture in the United States has a long history of romanticizing and eulogizing soldiers and police officers, a tradition that extends to Israeli soldiers, who are frequently endowed with superhuman strength and overzealous humanity. David is an example of a sensitive Israeli soldier, one incapable of violence. His presence in the West Bank is thus a mystery, but his reasonableness and personal charms render him a hero to both Jew and Arab. His heroic qualities justify his status as an occupier. David represents yet another colonial fantasy, that of the benign soldier. The benign soldier can earn the respect of his colonized subjects. He is never there for any reason of oppression. He romances his subject women and wins their approval. He handles the irrationality of his subjects with unusual patience. If they are lucky, they will learn crucial life lessons from him.

West Bank Story has a dark heart disguised by a sunny disposition. It is proactive art, hoping to teach its viewers that the Israel-Palestine conflict is not interminable. Yet its inveterate message of colonial absolution is more detrimental to resolving the conflict than the rightwing propaganda it purports to rectify. The film evinces the most arrogant of conceits, the belief that a colonizer is entitled to the adoration of those he has dispossessed without doing anything to earn it. Even its feel-good moments reify the deep violence of Israel's founding: at the end of the movie, the Jewish and Palestinian characters seek fellowship over cuisine such as falafel and hummus, food items appropriated from Arabs by Israelis who claim them as their own, to the profound frustration of the Palestinians. Thus *West Bank Story* does little more than present an unintended irony: the Jewish characters want to come closer to the Palestinians, but the only way they might realistically accomplish this goal is by leaving the Palestinians alone.

Munich: A Prayer for Peace of Mind

"You should make no mistake: I am not attacking Israel with this film. In no way, shape, or form am I doing that," *Munich* director Steven Spielberg proclaims in the DVD interview. Never has an artist uttered a truer statement. *Munich* is Spielberg's ballyhooed "prayer for peace," but, as in *West Bank Story*, its moral and philosophical recommendations actually ensure that peace will remain elusive. Aside from being morally troublesome and politically tendentious, *Munich* also has the distinction of being a dreadful film.

Spielberg gained his fame directing fun and adventurous Hollywood fare such as *Jurassic Park*, *Indiana Jones*, and *E.T.* Sometime in the early nineties, he developed a pang of liberal guilt and has since produced or directed a number of socially conscious movies like *Amistad*, *Saving Private Ryan*, *Schindler's List*, and *Munich*. With the exception of *Schindler's List*, an above-average movie, all of Spielberg's ostensibly serious work shares heavy-handed exposition, overwrought dialogue, and nugatory moralism. *Munich* purports to be a profound moral exposé, but it lacks any of the subtlety necessary to generate discussion. It informs viewers of what they ought to believe, instead. Spielberg faithfully reproduces the heart of darkness motif that we saw Cornel West promulgate in Chapter 3. The Jews experience an unprecedented moral crisis in their encounter with Palestinians, who perform incomprehensible levels of violence. The Palestinians exist only to frame this Jewish crisis of consciousness; they are never themselves moral agents. *Munich* assumes that their violence is unjust and irrational. The Israelis grapple with the depths of human brutality into which the Palestinians have forced them. As in Cornel West's lament, the Palestinians exist to corrupt Jewish purity.

The movie begins with silent Palestinians ready to attack the athletes' village in Munich in 1972. Spielberg then interjects the usual footage and news broadcasts, culminating in the injudicious German commando raid that resulted in the deaths of all eleven Israeli athletes. Already the film has problems, even before it transitions into the behind-the-scenes narrative meant to give the audience an insider's view of counterterrorism. The Palestinians who kidnapped the Israeli athletes, naming themselves Black September after the September 1970 expulsion of the Palestine Liberation Organization (PLO) from Jordan, were adamant in their determination not to murder the athletes, and evidence has surfaced that the Israeli athletes were killed by overzealous and incompetent German commandos.[2] No matter what actually happened in Munich, the representation of the Palestinian perpetrators by Spielberg is riddled with historical inaccuracy and high-minded exposition at the expense of an honest exploration of political violence in the Israel-Palestine conflict. In fact, Spielberg proffers imagery that is deeply jingoistic, as he does with the outsize American flag in *Saving Private Ryan* contextualizing all notions of heroism.

Munich is more egregious: Spielberg depicts Palestinians cheering upon the massacre of the Israeli athletes, imagery that by now is clichéd and prejudicial. At the end of the film, after the requisite terrorists have been liquidated, Spielberg cuts to an image of the twin towers on the Manhattan skyline as a solemn coda to the psychodrama viewers just witnessed. The conflation is unmistakable: the Israeli battle against Palestinian terrorists is indivisible from the United States' post-9/11 engagements in a Muslim world that has challenged Americans' sense of moral innocence and exposed their own dark hearts. In the interview accompanying the DVD, Spielberg makes it clear that he is interested not in the moral implications of violence against Arabs and Muslims but in finding a more efficient and guiltless way to fight terrorism. Just as Israelis have been lamenting the erosion of their national soul for many decades, American liberals have been mourning the degradation of the United States' virtue since 9/11. Spielberg puts the two laments together in a neat package of mutually constitutive military aggression. No matter how conscientious the Western protectors of higher values, the specter of dark barbarity always threatens. One of the Mossad agents in *Munich* questions their pursuit of Palestinian terrorists: "Did we accomplish anything at all? All the men we killed were replaced by worse." The West cannot approach Arabs peacefully, for Arabs understand only violence. And it cannot approach Arabs violently, for violence only makes Arabs more barbaric. Such is the moral crisis at the center of *Munich*.

In the wake of the Munich massacre, Israel assembled a secret Mossad unit to track down and assassinate the Palestinians responsible for planning it. The unit was dispatched on the order of Prime Minister Golda Meir, who in the film delivers a dramatic monologue: "These people, they're sworn to destroy us. Forget peace for now. We have to show them we're strong. We have laws. We represent civilization. I don't know who these maniacs are and where they come from. Palestinians. They're not recognizable." She concludes, "Every civilization finds it necessary to negotiate compromises with its own values." Meir's monologue includes a matronly countenance toward a slightly befuddled Avner (Eric Bana), an inexperienced soldier tasked with leading the classified unit in charge of exterminating Palestinians. This maternalism plays a central role throughout the film.

Before I enter into that analysis, I discuss a few rhetorical elements of interest in Meir's speech. For those familiar with the history of the Israel-Palestine conflict, Meir's confusion about the origin of Palestinians is curious, as they are indigenous to the land that foreign Jews settled. Meir, on the other hand, was born in Milwaukee, Wisconsin. The scene is a typical example of Spielberg's heavy-handedness. Meir suggests that the Palestinians are innately different than Jews, that there is something profoundly different about their moral caliber. She recapitulates all of the central mythologies of the dark heart motif: an inherently good society faces a bewildering enemy whose lack of principles and disrespect of human life pull the good society unwittingly into a military engagement that challenges all it holds morally sacred. The good society always emerges from this dark quagmire, but less innocent and schooled in the ways of the uncivilized. The good society's subsequent violence is thus the fault of its contact with subaltern evil. Important factors are usually absent from this dark heart motif: the act of colonization is continuous violence; it is inevitably the good society that introduces heretofore unknown brutality into its intercultural engagements; the objectionable behavior of the maniacs is explicable on both moral and strategic grounds. These complicating factors are inconvenient to the central narrative with which Spielberg works. That narrative relies on mythology to generate a visceral identification with the superior mores of Western civilization.

Meir is the matron of the anguished colonizer. Her presence as the mother figure of Spielberg's psychodrama evolves into a running motif. In *Munich*, Israel is a stern but loving parental figure to which all Jews have a complex but atavistic relationship. Israel's children are called upon by the mother to fulfill her existential desires and to return to the metonymical womb of the homeland, the only place on earth where a Jew can be safe and comforted. Avner rehearses this dynamic as both a parent and child. At the end of the film, after he has murdered his quota of Palestinians, he plays the good, anguished father, breaking down in tears as he beholds his baby daughter. The scene is typical Spielberg pathos, but this time distended into a particular symbolic context. Just as his mother has sacrificed for him, Avner has sacrificed for his daughter. Thus a peculiar form of tribal devotion binds intergenerational Jews to the idea of Israel. The gendered teleology of this devotion informs an age-old colonial paradigm of the alien landscape as a site of impregnation and birth. The process is arduous and often painful, but it is a necessary dimension of individual self-realization through the construction of a national identity.

Avner's relationship with his mother, played by Gila Almagor, is especially overwrought with the anxieties of existential alienation and maternal sublimation. When Avner is conflicted over his actions on behalf of Israel, his mother tells him, "I didn't die [in the Holocaust,] because I came here. Everyone who died died wanting this. We had to take it because none will ever give it to us: a place to be a Jew among Jews, subject to no one. Whatever it took, whatever it takes, we have a place on earth . . . at last." This passage fulfills a portentous observation Avner's wife, Daphna (Ayelet Zurer), teasingly offers him earlier in the film after a round of intercourse: "Now you think Israel is your mother." Much of Avner's moral angst arises from Israel's being irresistible but elusive in the most basic manner of Lacanian psychoanalysis. Avner wants to be loved and accepted but feels that his actions preclude him from deserving maternal love and acceptance. It is up to his daughter, wife, and mother to affirm his violence as a patriot on behalf of their collective national family. The film's coadunation of Avner's mother figures and Israel is explicit. At one point—again, amid intercourse, as if to telegraph Avner's creepy neediness—Avner confides to Daphna, "You're the only home I ever had." Avner's mother provides him this much-needed affirmation: "I am proud of what you are doing." She becomes coterminous with the nation when the jovial soldiers who pick up Avner from the airport tell him, "It's an honor to meet you."

All of these psychological elements are in conversation with the central issue of Jewish purity and its struggle to remain virtuous amid the corrupting presence of Palestinians. This issue haunts the Mossad hit squad as it undertakes its high-tech and sometimes perilous murders. One member of the squad, a particularly sensitive bomb expert named Robert (Mathieu Kassovitz), finally caves to the pressure, leading to this exchange with Avner:

ROBERT: All this blood comes back to us.
AVNER: Eventually it will work. Even if it takes years we'll beat them.
ROBERT: We're Jews, Avner. Jews don't do wrong because our enemies do wrong.
AVNER: We can't afford to be that decent anymore.
ROBERT: I don't know that we ever were that decent. Suffering thousands of years of hatred doesn't make you decent. We're supposed to be righteous. That's a beautiful thing. That's Jewish. That's my soul.

Robert reinvents the self-congratulatory narrative of those who confront the darkness within themselves. This confrontation never happens in the confines of civilized society; it must occur through contact with agents of barbarism whose indecency gradually erodes the pristine soul of the civilized subject. In *Munich*, this motif has a specific geopolitical context, one in which the timeless humanity of the Jewish people is manifested through Zionism, which sometimes compels its devotees to do evil in order to do good. The Palestinians have no agency in this narrative; they are merely dark backdrops to a psychodrama in which they have no role other than as anonymous and uncivil objects of Jewish self-discovery.

This story reinforces longstanding mythologies. The Israeli agents go out of their way to spare civilians, putting themselves at grave risk in the process. They reflect forlornly about their actions, sometimes getting into arguments. One of the agents, Steve (Daniel Craig), proclaims, "Unless we learn to act like [the Palestinians], we will never defeat them," to which the more liberal Carl (Ciarán Hinds) replies, "We act like them all the time. You think the Palestinians invented bloodshed? How do you think we got control of the land, by being nice?" Carl's reproach is the extent of the Israelis' acknowledgment of their own violence. Carl's point of view loses, however. Steve attacks him and he eventually dies, his sensitive consciousness following him to the grave. Steve, on the other hand, lives long enough to proclaim, "The only blood that matters to me is Jewish blood," a viewpoint that ultimately prevails. An interesting feature of this Israeli soul-searching, one that underlies all dark heart themes, is its unacknowledged contradictions. While it is Palestinian savagery that contextualizes the Israelis' coerced brutality, their soul-searching is facilitated through their performance of violent actions. This exposes a deep ethical flaw in epistemologies of colonization. It is not just the violence of the native that foregrounds the decline of the colonizer's virtues; the colonizer's virtues are inherently violent, necessitating an entanglement with violence in order to induce introspection and catharsis. As in all such entanglements, *Munich* affirms the colonizer's violence as imperative and just.

This imperative and just violence can always be rationalized as extrinsic through invocation of native violence, no matter its nature or origin. Anytime Avner becomes hesitant, he evokes mental images of the Munich murders, which provide him the necessary fortitude to undertake his string of assassinations. In fact, the movie begins with this sort of imagery, showing a pensive Avner at the beginning of his mission, staring into the dark portal of an airplane window the camera focuses on and zooms in to. The portal evolves from a screen of solid black to a backdrop for Avner's visualization of Munich, where Palestinian terrorists mowed down innocent Israelis. Avner comes to learn that, as his private intelligence contact Louis (Mathieu Amalric) says, "It costs dearly, but home always does." If there is to be an Israel, violence is required. As long as Palestinians are around, they can be blamed for dubious Jewish behavior.

The struggle to remain civilized in the face of their incivility creates the film's central paradox, that modernity entails the same bloodiness it purports to transcend. Spielberg and scriptwriters Eric Roth and Tony Kushner infuse the paradox with a yearning for acceptance, a constant feature of Israel since its inception. If the mother figure illuminates a deep need for a homeland through the metaphor of a womb, the father figure represents an earned legitimacy for Israel. Avner exists in the shadow of his father, an invisible character who is for unexplained reasons an imprisoned national hero. Avner's goal is to live up to his father's patriotism while retaining a moral center. Avner develops a relationship with Louis's boss, a mysterious intelligence merchant who is adamantly unaffiliated to any national cause. This merchant is named Papa, yet another bit of explicit symbolism. Even though Papa purports to be an anarchist, he has a tender spot for Israel, telling Avner, "The world has been rough with you, with your tribe. It is right to respond roughly to such treatment." Avner comes to trust Papa but can never attain any sort of intimacy with him. Papa reminds him, "You could have been my son, but you're not." The fatherless Avner must interpolate his paternal abandonment into the meaningful task of nation-building. When he is not sublimating his desires for maternal affirmation into the ugly work of ethnonationalism, he spends time accepting Papa's obvious but somehow cruel observation by positioning Israel as a paternal geography of his birthright.

Perhaps nothing exemplifies *Munich*'s strange psychology better than the scene in which members of the unit shoot a treacherous woman who is not Palestinian but seen to be in league with them. The men shoot the woman while she is wearing a bathrobe, ignoring her sexual overtures. The force of the bullets flips open her robe, exposing her breasts and vagina as she lies dead. Avner solemnly covers her vagina with her robe. "No, leave it," the oldest member of the unit, Hans (Hanns Zischler), says, flipping the robe back open to render the dead woman exposed. Later, Hans introspects, "It's not that I wish we hadn't killed her. I wish I had closed up her house coat." Steve consoles him, "Yeah, but you weren't yourself." The movie's convoluted ethics emerge in full force here, as the murder is conceptualized as righteous but the nudity as inappropriate, a sign of disrespect that compromises Hans's honor. In moments of passion, the Israelis are sometimes compelled to misbehave, but only in alternate states of consciousness and in the presence of treachery and evil. The woman's body is symbolic of an intimacy forged in violence through which the Palestinians are subsumed in a naked desire to kill and evoke the darkness deep inside others. The Palestinians assume the murdered woman's tragic persona of a figure who was delivered the end she deserved, but with an overzealousness arising from the intensity of righteousness.

The film's cinematographic darkness paradoxically illuminates its focus on the moral ambiguities of colonial violence. *Munich* does a fabulous job of absolving the colonizer of violence by conferring its foundational presence to the native and then attributing colonial brutality to the quagmire initiated by the native's innate barbarity. The only reason Palestinians exist in *Munich* is for Jews to undertake a silly and sanctimonious conversation about the limits of their inherent goodness. The darkness of many scenes and the shadows constantly moving about the film's peripheries represent the irritating Palestinian evilness from which the Jews must salvage the inspiriting lightness of civility. Unfortunately for viewers, Spielberg isn't nearly as talented a storyteller as Conrad's Marlowe, and way too much of a pedant to do the interesting thing and disappear into an impenetrable forest as his unacknowledged hero, Kurtz, did.

Waltz with Bashir: Dancing in the Darkness

Although *Munich* and *Waltz with Bashir* are quite similar (verging on analogous) thematically, they are very different structurally and visually. *Waltz with Bashir*, first of all, is a much better movie, displaying wonderful cinematography and an impressive technical production. Its visuals are often stunning and presented with unusual skill, like its contemporary *Persepolis*'s, an adaptation of a graphic novel. Its writer and director, Ari Folman, is much less didactic and overwrought than Spielberg and offers more engaging moral and philosophical nuance. *Waltz with Bashir* nevertheless evinces some fundamental problems. Its most conspicuous problem is its reiteration of basal dark heart motifs that Folman might have usefully complicated were his political worldview more discerning than what he manages to display in the film.

Waltz with Bashir is ostensibly about the 1982 massacre in Sabra and Shatila, but Sabra and Shatila, like Arabs in general, are merely a pretext for disquietude about Israeli guilt and ontological insecurity. The film's presentation of the massacre is unjustifiably attenuated. Let us take a look at the facts of that massacre. On September 16, 1982, following the murder of Phalange Party leader Bashir Gemayel by unknown assailants, Phalangist militia, comprising Maronite Christians, entered the refugee camp of Shatila and the adjoining neighborhood of Sabra (not in fact a refugee camp) and proceeded to slaughter approximately three thousand Palestinian civilians over the course of three days. The massacre included the point-blank murder of entire families and the transportation of civilians in trucks to be murdered en masse. Although *Waltz with Bashir* depicts these events with relative accuracy, it whitewashes Israel's role in the massacre. The Israeli military and the many soldiers surrounding the camps had knowledge of the ongoing massacre. Evidence shows that Israel colluded with the Phalange, both in planning the massacre and in facilitating the Phalange's disposal of bodies. Sabra and Shatila was an atrocity for which the Phalange and its ally Israel bear equal moral responsibility no matter the apportionment of actual physical participation. An important factor to keep in mind is Israel's responsibility for thousands of civilian deaths during the course of its 1982 Lebanon invasion.[3]

Waltz with Bashir acknowledges some of Israel's responsibility and hints at IOF participation in the massacre, but it elides the matter of culpability by transforming the massacre into a series of tormented individual memories that taken together comprise a reflective but confident Israeli national consciousness. According to their portrayal in *Waltz with Bashir*, Sabra and Shatila are exemplary hearts of darkness, providing a setting for the sort of self-reflection that only the barbarism of dark culture can evoke. A curious feature of the film is its widespread reception as critical of Israel. In fact, *Waltz with Bashir* is a critique of individual journeys of culpability and absolution without adding up to any type of cohesive interrogation of national practice or identity. The movie says very little about Israel, and even less about the actions that might cast Israel in a negative light. If anything, Israel is portrayed as self-aware and heroic, as against the anonymous masses of unrepentant and mindless Arabs. It is for this reason that *Waltz with Bashir* received Israeli government support, promoted as part of Israel's effort at cultural agitprop in embassies and consulates around the world. Folman notes that "the film became a darling of the establishment."[4]

Indeed, the *Jewish Telegraphic Agency* explains,

> The Israeli response, according to Folman, was positive for two reasons: It made Israel look like a tolerant country, allowing soldiers to talk openly about their experiences in the war, and when it was screened in Europe it made many people there realize for the first time that it wasn't the Israeli troops that committed the 1982 Sabra and Shatila massacres.
>
> "They didn't pull the trigger; it was the Christian regime," Folman said. "And this is the type of propaganda the Israeli government couldn't buy for money. So they kept sending the movie out."[5]

Elsewhere, Folman has noted that the film "did good" by showing European audiences that "it was a Christian regime that did the [Sabra and Shatila] massacre and not Israeli troops."[6] Folman has also been quoted claiming that "one thing for sure is that the Christian Phalangist militiamen were fully responsible for the massacre. The Israeli soldiers had nothing to do with it."[7]

Now that we have illustrated the film's establishmentarian credentials and its sterling propaganda value based on the testimony of its writer, producer, and director, it is salubrious to dispense with the fantasy that it is an antiwar or pro-Arab statement and instead analyze its actual content. One noteworthy feature of the film is its palpable disingenuousness. Its story is straightforward. Folman, an autobiographical character, meets with a friend, Boaz, who served in Israel's 1982 invasion of Lebanon and confides in Folman about a recurring nightmare he has about his murder of twenty-six dogs that would bark and warn "terrorists" about the approach of Israeli soldiers. This meeting gradually uncovers Folman's own repressed memories of the war, particularly his role in the Sabra and Shatila massacre. Through a series of conversations with army comrades and notable public figures, Folman pieces together his time in Lebanon, finally absolving himself of any responsibility for the murder of innocents. He is horrified by the slaughter of Arabian horses and Palestinian refugees, but as far as he is concerned he had nothing to do with it. He merely chanced upon these horrors and now has to deal with the trauma of his role as witness. In the movie, the dogs and horses receive more sympathy than Arab casualties.

I deem the narrative disingenuous because Folman asks viewers to accept a portrayal of Israeli military naïveté and incompetence that doesn't cohere with the facts of its behavior in Lebanon. If one believes Folman's account, the IOF is one of the stupidest and most ragtag militaries in the world. I do not doubt that the IOF, like any other bureaucracy, has its share of hubris and idiocy despite its massive budget and technological sophistication, but it was not the confused and destitute outfit in Lebanon that is shown in *Waltz with Bashir*. It was in reality a massive force capable of efficient destruction and the infliction of widespread civilian casualties. Even if individual soldiers such as Folman and his pals may have had little sense of their situations (a dubious proposition), their ignorance did not extend throughout the IOF brass, as the film suggests. During the Sabra and Shatila massacre, for instance, Folman renders Ariel Sharon's knowledge and involvement ambiguous. The film indicates that his complicity was a possibility but not a certainty, although all historical evidence points to the contrary.[8] Moreover, Folman didn't appear to understand why he and fellow soldiers were shooting flares over Sabra and Shatila. When he finally realizes twenty years later that the flares were actually helping the Phalange with their operation he shudders with recognition but still never assigns himself any blame, thus recapitulating the same astonishing ignorance he expects viewers to believe a second time.

Ignorance is the film's most consistent motif. Folman the nineteen-year-old soldier never knows what's happening; nor do his friends and higher-ups. A pervasive obliviousness attends to Sabra and Shatila as it occurs: "It seemed natural," Folman observes about the mobilization of Phalange troops; the Palestinian civilians being taken out of the camp are traveling to "an unknown destination." Any Israeli blame for the massacre belongs to completely anonymous military bureaucrats. Folman explains, "The massacre was carried out by Christian Phalangists," during which the Israeli soldiers "didn't realize they were witnessing a genocide." The use of the term "genocide" to describe the massacre is potentially seditious in Israel, but it is welcomed in this case because it puts even greater distance between the Israeli occupiers and the Maronite killers. According to Folman's recovered memory, in contravention of all historical documentation, it is the Israeli soldiers who put a halt to the massacre. Folman keeps banging home his innocence. His long-time friend Ori Sivan convinces him that he's fundamentally different from the Phalangists: "You didn't carry out the massacre." The main function of Folman's creepy friend Carmi Cna'an, a wealthy falafel vendor in Holland, is to constantly reinforce this innocence. Carmi attempts to cast light on Israel's presence in Lebanon, but he doesn't offer a single description of the invasion without claiming fear or ignorance as the motive of all IOF actions.

Ori extends the language of genocide in what is supposed to be the movie's seminal bit of dialogue. Upon Folman's recovery of memory, he is tasked with confronting the consequences of his presence at Sabra and Shatila. Instead, his therapist merely accommodates his desire for easy absolution: "Unwillingly, you took on the role of a Nazi." This sentence is remarkable for its invocation of a radical viewpoint that is disavowed before it is even completed. To say that Israeli soldiers acted as Nazis in Lebanon is profoundly suggestive on both political and symbolic levels. Such a declaration would indicate that Israel has assumed the character of the Jews' most brutal oppressors, on whose atrocities the state of Israel justifies its existence (and many of its controversial policies). Any assertion that conflates Israel with Nazism discredits the very idea of a Jewish nationalism because of the moral implications of a purportedly liberatory state reproducing the same oppression from which Jews escaped. To conflate Israel with Nazism also belies the promise of enlightenment and democracy. Fortunately for Folman, Ori didn't actually make or endorse such a declaration. He renders

Folman's participation in the massacre "unwilling," a qualification that severely tests the viewer's credulity. By not acting directly as a Nazi, but by unwillingly taking on the role of a Nazi, Folman is doubly absolved of his complicity in the massacre. How might one unwillingly take on the role of a Nazi? Is such a performance even possible? These are some of the questions that arise in Ori Sivan's remarkable observation. Were the German soldiers who secured the perimeter of the Warsaw Ghetto in 1943 free of any guilt for the deaths of thirteen thousand Jews? Were the two platoons of Charlie Company that cordoned off the Vietnamese village of My Lai in 1968 while American soldiers murdered over five hundred civilians innocent of responsibility? We have to consider these formulations as real possibilities if Folman and other Israeli soldiers can be successfully absolved of their role in the Sabra and Shatila massacre. Folman is asking viewers to accept the proposition that a proclaimed (but not proven) ignorance is a valid reason to excuse participation in genocide.[9] He also surmises that only those who carry guns and shoot others are responsible for murder, as opposed to those who facilitate murder, as he and his buddies did in Beirut. I submit that it is infeasible both morally and ontologically to be an unwilling Nazi; the unwilling Nazi is an oxymoron whose attendant elements do not comprise a realistic figure. The very act of behaving as a Nazi requires the sort of agency that Folman refuses to own. He shifts the blame to Arabs instead.

Despite its considerable ethical points of debate, I do not want to lose sight of the fact that *Waltz with Bashir* is art and that Folman's reluctance to adequately confront his recovered memory makes it a comely but underachieving film, one that is attenuated and thematically superficial. Ori tells Folman, "Memory is dynamic. It's alive." This claim is true psychologically and has provided much inspiration for theoretical analysis, but it doesn't provide any depth to *Waltz with Bashir* because it doesn't describe Folman's relationship to his lost or recovered memories. Folman's memory is actually static and it dies the moment Ori convinces him that he did nothing wrong in Lebanon. "The massacre frightens you, makes you uneasy," Ori points out to Folman, but Folman is uneasy not because of brutality and bloodiness but because he is afraid of assuming any moral culpability for the massacre. The main problem with the film, then, is not merely one of an exclusively Israeli point of view but an absence of empathy by Folman and other Israeli characters for the people they killed and helped to kill in Lebanon. *Waltz with Bashir* tells an incomplete story. It eviscerates the usefulness of psychoanalysis. It exchanges insight for a cheap propaganda value of which Folman is visibly proud.

This isn't to say that *Waltz with Bashir* lacks profundity. It uses the imagery of water as a complex metaphor and has lots to say, perhaps unwittingly, about the interaction of sex and war. Yet these moments are overshadowed by a dogmatic narrative. Very few critics have identified the movie's peremptory qualities, but *Waltz with Bashir* proffers a version of Sabra and Shatila that could have been plagiarized from the Kahan Commission Report (KCR). The KCR has an interesting history. It was released in 1983 by a committee headed by Yitzhak Kahan, president of Israel's Supreme Court, which determined that "the massacre at Sabra and Shatilla [*sic*] was carried out by a Phalangist unit, acting on its own but its entry was known to Israel. No Israeli was directly responsible for the events which occurred in the camps."[10] Instead, the KCR stressed that certain members of the military apparatus, such as Ariel Sharon, bore "indirect responsibility" for the massacre. Thus entered into the parlance of modernity the notion of "indirect responsibility," a rationale for moral ambiguity where none is necessary thanks to the efficacy of a deeply exculpatory document. The parallels between the "unwilling Nazi" and "indirect responsibility" are manifest, as is the general sentiment that Israel must be absolved of its criminality while maintaining the pretense of a self-critical liberal democracy. Prime Minister Menachem Begin circumvented all of the histrionics by simply declaring, "Goyim kill goyim, and they come to hang the Jews."[11]

The main lack in the KCR that can be found in *Waltz with Bashir* is the film's use of labyrinthine symbolism. Folman is especially concerned with the physical and philosophical qualities of water. Carmi spends time in the ocean, as do other characters. Zahava Soloman, Folman's therapist, explains the preponderance of water throughout the film when she informs Ari that the sea symbolizes fear and feelings in dreams. *Waltz with Bashir* is thus a story about emotions evoked by memory and the anxieties that result when they are repressed. The sea transports the characters to war and then entraps them in Lebanon, but it offers freedom and diversion. It embodies the endless fluctuation of their ambiguity. The pervasiveness of sexual desire intersects with the water motif.

When Carmi swims into the Mediterranean to escape Arab soldiers, he is transported atop the vagina of a white, blond woman, oversize and ethereal in the hazy memory of a stoned Carmi. The presence of this quintessentially Western woman in Lebanon's civil war is an unexamined fantasy of fulfillment through a safe sensuality that further distances Arabs from the spaces invaded by Israel. Carmi is oblivious to the existence of his sexual desire, conferring such phenomena to the realm of tribal Arab politics. He tells Ari about the Phalangist reaction to Bashir Gemayel, head of the party and eponym of the movie, described by one Israeli military commander as "a brother, an ally, a Christian." Gemayel's unsolved murder was a major impetus of the Sabra and Shatila massacre.[12] Carmi recalls about Gemayel's militia, "I think they even felt an eroticism for him. Totally erotic." This eroticism led them to exact revenge in "a perverse way." Carmi concludes, "This was about family honor, which runs deep." Although Carmi is working from a Rolodex of venerable Orientalist stereotypes, his description applies just as well to the Israeli soldiers, though Folman chooses to not pursue this angle. Phalange ruthlessness and its relationship with Phalangist sexual neuroses are an unexamined foil to Israeli erotic dysfunction. Carmi merely projects onto the Phalange all of the qualities about which he and Ari are in denial. Carmi himself is on a quest to get laid, enthralled as he is by the exotic qualities of the Eastern landscape and its mysterious women. With his oceanic images of outsize nude white women, he illuminates the perverted fantasies that continue to afflict Ari and other veterans even after they recover their memories. The most conspicuous moment of honesty is the scene in which Ari stays at an opulent mansion overtaken by Israeli soldiers who engage in various forms of debauchery and whose indolent commander sits around watching pornography. Otherwise, all Israeli dysfunction is transferred to the nameless, and almost completely unseen, Arab antagonists.

At one point in the movie a persistent television reporter, Ron Ben-Yisha, describes the sounds of Sabra and Shatila: "It sounded like a Native American archery range." All of the problems with *Waltz with Bashir* become apparent upon the delivery of this line. The sound of an American Indian archery range is yet another colonialist fantasy, an imagining of something that doesn't exist outside the metropolitan gaze. The quaint idea of an American Indian archery range further absolves the agents of violence in Sabra and Shatila by comparing them to the romantic Indian of Hollywood vintage. An American Indian archery range might bespeak savagery, but it is a savagery of the variety that intimates a mindless or mysterious violence, one that the modern Western consumer, such as the Israeli, is unable to fully understand. In Beirut, the Israelis have entered into a strange world that beggars their civilized imaginations. This strange world is murky and elusive, nestled into their psyches so deeply that it arouses emotions that would otherwise be inaccessible. They must then confront their darkest selves, those profound essences that, when evoked, make them momentarily resemble the Arabs that so frighten them.

Even though all the action in *Waltz with Bashir* leads to the Sabra and Shatila massacre, this ostensibly climactic event isn't the point of the movie. The point of the movie is that Israelis ought to be careful lest they arouse their inherent potential to become as savage as their enemies. This fate can be avoided by eschewing hubristic imperialism and staying within the confines of modernity as it is embodied by Israel. For all of its accolades, there is little of note about *Waltz with Bashir* beyond its excellent animation. Its story was already told by the Israeli government in the Kahan Commission Report. Its main conflict has been narrated so many times that it lacks as much pertinence as it does originality. Indeed, the most progressive thing about the film is its approval of smoking marijuana. It is telling that Ari smokes joints only in the Netherlands, where he is breaking no law.

Dark Hearts and Tortured Souls

One can learn much about Zionism by watching the movies that explore its internal conflicts. No matter its politics or level of devotion to Israel, this sort of movie attempts to resolve the innate contradiction of Israel as a purported liberal democracy deeply ensconced in modernity as against its origin and present as an ethnocentric and militarized state. If it appears that these films inevitably reproduce this contradiction it is because the contradiction's reproduction is inevitable. No ethnonationalist movement can make its lofty and often humanistic rhetoric cohere with its exclusionary jurisprudence. The moral and philosophical space between these inconsistent phenomena is the site of change and conflict in the dark heart films, one of the reasons why they vary even as they remain tethered, sometimes inadvertently, to the same theme. The difference of quality in these films is to some degree subjective, although I argue that *Munich* fails to execute any of the basic criteria for a good movie. The other two films I discussed are at the very least passable as art, at times riveting or transcendent. Their quality is not the primary issue, however. The primary issue is the comparable fashion in which each film creates a distinctly Arab setting as the site of deep moral conflict over the nature of Zionism. Each film explores problems with the ideology but ultimately validates the basic goodness of Zionism. The unsavory elements of Zionism become the domain or responsibility of the Arab antagonist. Zionism would have fulfilled its humanistic and utopian promise were it not for the encounter with a hostile enemy whose barbarism evoked the same dormant quality in the colonizer.

The corrupting power of Palestinians has been a constant motif in Zionist art and politics. It is central to movies beyond the ones I have discussed in this chapter, such as *You Don't Mess with the Zohan*, *Lebanon*, and *Time of Favor*. Even *Exodus*, the classic Zionist narrative, invokes the corrupting presence of Arabs. Cinema was one of the earliest means for Zionist leaders of distributing propaganda. Today's Zionist films continue a tradition of self-reflection that cannot occur without the silent participation of proximal but otherworldly Palestinians. In many ways, the films I have examined in this chapter illuminate the centrality of the indigenous Palestinian population to the Holy Land, who represent a present absence that cannot be avoided, and that won't simply go away. Not only do these Palestinians evoke the darkness of the otherwise gentle Jewish soul, they constantly remind Jewish Israelis of the uglier necessities of their colonial enterprise. Although each film differs in quality and style, the films have in common an important central feature: they are unwilling to confront racism in a meaningful or systematic way, instead emphasizing the inevitability of evil as a means to the establishment of something that is fundamentally good. This evil is simply a simulacrum of the racism of ethnonationalism that is subsequently unexamined.

These films, like the broader political narratives with which they are contextualized, are fundamentally optimistic. The Israeli soul is constantly under attack by the barbarous forces representing premodernity, but it always manages to survive the savagery that confronts and devalues it. This survival occurs because of painful but necessary introspection, a confrontation of the darkness in the Israeli heart and the decline of its pristine soul. Ultimately, though, Israel's heart and soul avert the darkness introduced by Arabs, to whom it is congenital. As a result, Zionism has cultivated a thriving film industry, one that is steadfastly quixotic. Despite this industry's massive budget and technological sophistication, its films are entrapped in an unmoving ethics of black and white.

Epilogue

A Eulogy to Israel's Dead Soul

The anxious chattering guardians of national consciousness, composed of liberal writers and eager do-gooders, killed Israel's soul. They did not kill it through violence, however. They killed it by inventing it. This death isn't tragic. It is to be celebrated. Israel's soul needed to die if the many peoples of the Near East are to continue living.

By endowing a nation-state, the progenitor of militarism and technocracy, with the most abstract but sacred element of humanity, a soul, those fretting over Israel's encounters with darkness ensured its eternal soullessness. This paradox does not threaten Israel's future; it portends the safety and survival of the Jewish and Palestinian people. By insisting that nation-states have souls, we prevent ourselves from tending to the humans who subsist within the institutions. The nation-state does not procure a human soul. The nation-state circumscribes the human soul.

The murder of Israel's soul by its guardians has not led to the death of the state itself. That will happen when Israel becomes a democratic entity and not an ethnonationalist state. It is a valuable goal to pursue, for the survival of Palestinians, and perhaps of Jews, is contingent on the destruction of Israel's colonial apparatus—that is to say, the dissolution of Israel in its extant configuration and its reconstruction as a sovereign democracy for all of its citizens. Israel occupies a geography that has never been pristine or homogeneous.

Zionism's claims to the Palestinian past, then, are usually affectations of colonial violence in the present.

But we must not make the mistake of conceptualizing Israel's dead soul as a Christian-style redemption in which carnage and resurrection are requisite. Israel's dead soul is the affirmation of life through its long-overdue murder. Colonization harnesses racism and nurtures intemperate power. Its agents act on these ills with little consequence and often with little conscience. If evil deeds performed in the service of a nation-state can endow it with a soul, then the very idea of humanity is devalued. I feel as if I have a soul. I do not want my soul to have an ethereal or ontological association with Israel.

We can replace the sort of ethnonationalism that underlies Zionism with an internationalism that affirms all ways of being and eschews the reliance on biology to determine belonging. In the end, Zionism produces continuous abrogation of human rights. It compels its advocates to create a tenebrous fantasy world of ostensibly apolitical art and humane politics. In reality it actualizes the worst of corporate greed and ideological excess.

Do not mourn Israel's dead soul, then. Mourn instead those who suffer when Israel's soul is living.

Notes

Introduction

1. Ruthie Blum Leibowitz, "One on One: Rehab for an 'All-Consuming Peace Addiction,'" *Jerusalem Post*, 25 May 2009.

2. David Grossman, "Something to Mourn," *Ha'aretz*, 30 September 2009.

3. David Grossman, "After Netanyahu, Israel Is a Country about to Purge Itself," *Los Angeles Times*, 9 June 1999.

4. Richard Silverstein, "Killing Donkeys for Sport: Time-Honored IDF Tradition," 5 February 2009, available at http://www.richardsil verstein.com/tikun_olam/2009/02/05/killing-donkeys-for-sport-time-honored-idf-tradition/.

5. Yoram Hazony, *The Jewish State: The Struggle for Israel's Soul* (New York: Basic Books, 2001), 73.

6. Alon Hadar, "'We'll Never Be Normal,'" *Ha'aretz*, 12 January 2008.

7. Tsela Barr, "Israeli Soul Corrupted by 40 Years of Occupation," *Madison Capital Times*, 9 June 2007.

8. See, e.g., http://www.kirjasto.sci.fi/amichai.htm.

9. See, e.g., http://www.ynetnews.com/articles/0,7340,L-3554523,00 .html.

10. Cathy Young, "Israel Faces a Soul-Searching Double Standard," *Real Clear Politics*, 1 April 2009, available at http://www.realclearpolitics .com/articles/2009/04/israel_faces_a_soul_searching.html.

11. Ibid.

12. Antony Loewenstein, "How Occupation Has Corrupted Israel's Soul," *Antony Loewenstein*, 30 March 2008, available at http://antony loewenstein.com/2008/03/30/how-occupation-has-corrupted-israels-soul/.

13. Yossi Klein Halevi, "Israel's Gift to a Terrorized World," *Aish.com*, 2 February 2004, available at http://www.aish.com/jw/me/48906277.html.

14. For some historiography and analysis, see, e.g., Mohamed Heikal, *Secret Channels: The Inside Story of Arab-Israeli Peace Negotiations* (New York: HarperCollins, 1997); David Hirst, *The Gun and the Olive Branch: The Roots of Violence in the Middle East* (New York: Nation Books, 2003); Avi Shlaim, *The Iron Wall: Israel and the Arab World* (New York: Norton, 2001); Ilan Pappe, *The Ethnic Cleansing of Palestine* (Oxford: Oneworld Publications, 2007); Nur Masalha, *Expulsion of the Palestinians: The Concept of Transfer in Zionist Political Thought, 1882–1948* (Washington, DC: Institute for Palestine Studies, 1992); Walid Khalidi, *All that Remains: The Palestinian Villages Occupied and Depopulated by Israel in 1948* (Washington, DC: Institute for Palestine Studies, 2006); and Sami Hadawi, *Bitter Harvest: A Modern History of Palestine* (Northampton, MA: Interlink, 1998).

15. For detailed information about discrimination against Palestinian citizens of Israel, including numerous investigative reports, please see the website of Adalah: The Legal Center for Arab Minority Rights in Israel, available at http://www.adalah.org.

16. After a visit to Palestine, Tutu wrote, "I've been very deeply distressed in my visit to the Holy Land; it reminded me so much of what happened to us black people in South Africa. I have seen the humiliation of the Palestinians at checkpoints and roadblocks, suffering like us when young white police officers prevented us from moving about." Desmond Tutu, "Apartheid in the Holy Land," *Guardian* (London), 29 April 2002.

17. In 2006 Carter told the Canadian Broadcasting Corporation, "When Israel does occupy this territory deep within the West Bank, and connects the 200-or-so settlements with each other, with a road, and then prohibits the Palestinians from using that road, or in many cases even crossing the road, this perpetrates even worse instances of apartness, or apartheid, than we witnessed even in South Africa." Quoted in "Jimmy Carter: Israel's 'Apartheid' Policies Worse Than South Africa's," *Ha'aretz*, 11 December 2006.

18. George Gilder, *The Israel Test* (Minneapolis, MN: Richard Vigilante Books, 2009).

19. See, e.g., Iris Marion Young, *Global Challenges* (Cambridge: Polity, 2006); Andrea Smith, *Conquest* (Boston: South End Press, 2005); and Chandra Talpade Mohanty, *Feminism Without Borders* (Durham, NC: Duke University Press, 2003).

Chapter 1

1. See, e.g., Alexander Cockburn and Jeffrey St. Clair, eds., *The Politics of Anti-Semitism* (Oakland, CA: AK Press, 2003); Norman Finkelstein, *Beyond Chutzpah* (Berkeley: University of California Press, 2006); Walter Laqueur, *The Changing Face of Anti-Semitism* (Oxford: Oxford University Press, 2008); and Bernard Harrison, *The Resurgence of Anti-Semitism* (Lanham, MD: Rowman and Littlefield, 2006).

2. Information on Hillel's budget was procured through a GuideStar search. The budget figure comes from Hillel's 2007 Internal Revenue Service (IRS) Form 990.

3. Hillel, "Imagining a More Civil Society: The University and Jewish Community," Summit Packet, 2008, pp. 4, 2.

4. Hillel, "Hillel's Vision for Israel on Campus," available at http://www.hillel.org/israel/campus_vision.htm.

5. Ibid.

6. The statement is available at http://www.hillel.org/israel/default.

7. Iris Marion Young, *Global Challenges* (Cambridge: Polity, 2007), 26.

8. Ibid.

9. Nur Masalha, *The Bible and Zionism* (London: Zed, 2007), 2.

10. Joel Olson, *The Abolition of White Democracy* (Minneapolis: University of Minnesota Press, 2004), xx.

11. For more information about the attack on the USS *Liberty*, see James Scott, *The Attack on the* Liberty (New York: Simon and Schuster, 2009).

12. The mission statement is available at http://www.mcp.vt.edu/.

13. The mission statement is available at http://www.radford.edu/diverse/about_us.htm.

14. The mission statement is available at http://yalecollege.yale.edu/content/iac.

15. The mission statement is available at http://msc.wisc.edu/msc/.

16. This statement is available at http://www.microsoft.com/about/diversity/monthly.mspx.

17. The statement is available at http://www.thecoca-colacompany.com/citizenship/workplace_culture.html.

18. This statement is available at http://www.fox.com/diversity/.

19. The video is available at http://maxblumenthal.com/feeling-the-hate-in-jerusalem/.

20. Aviram Zino, "Racism in Israel on the Rise," *Yediot Aharonot*, 8 December 2007.

21. Ibid.

22. The quote is available at http://www.presstv.ir/detail.aspx?id=101852&sectionid=351020202.

23. See, e.g., http://www.ynetnews.com/articles/0,7340,L-3723755, 00.html.

24. The report is available at http://www.jcrcboston.org/assets/files/ A-PAPER-ON-ETHOPIAN.pdf

Chapter 2

1. Audrey Shabbas, "Coalition Raises Doubts About ADL," *Washington Report on Middle East Affairs*, June 1989, p. 37.

2. ADL 2008 Annual Report, p. 33, available at http://www.adl.org/ annual_report/Annual_Report_2008.pdf.

3. Ibid., 33.

4. IRS Form 990, p. 4.

5. Ibid., Part V-A.

6. Ibid., Schedule A.

7. Ibid.

8. Matt Isaacs, "Spy vs Spite," *San Francisco Weekly*, 2 February 2000.

9. ADL 2008 Annual Report, pp. 4–5.

10. See, e.g., the 2009 report of the Palestinian Center for Human Rights, *War Crimes against Children*, which notes that, during Israel's Operation Cast Lead, "1,414 Palestinians were killed, including 313 children. The evidence obtained by PCHR strongly indicates that the overwhelming majority of these victims were civilians." Available at http:// www.pchrgaza.org/files/Reports/English/pdf_spec/War%20Crimes%20 Against%20Children%20Book.pdf.

11. ADL 2008 Annual Report, p. 5.

12. See, e.g., "Anti-Semitic Incidents Decline for Fourth Straight Year in U.S., According to Annual ADL Audit," available at http://www.adl .org/PresRele/ASUS_12/5537_12.htm.

13. Daniel Edelson, "Report: Global anti-Semitism Declined in 2008," *Yehidot Aharanot*, 20 April 2009, available at http://www.ynet .co.il/english/articles/0,7340,L-3703686,00.html.

14. Here are four examples: Ivan Ivanov, a Bulgarian Jew in Brooklyn was arrested in January 2008, for numerous instances of spray painting anti-Semitic graffiti on houses, vehicles, and synagogues. The *New York Times* reported that Ivanov was trained by the Mossad. See, e.g., http:// www.jewishtulsa.org/local_includes/downloads/23167.pdf p, 3. In 2007 numerous swastikas that turned up on the campus of George Washington University were ultimately attributed to a Jewish student, Sarah Marshak, who was caught on tape drawing one on her dormitory room door. See, e.g., http://jta.org/news/article/2007/11/06/105127/swastikasuniversity.

In 2008 an eighteen-year-old German woman received a civic courage award for having survived a hate crime in which a swastika was carved into her leg—but she had carved the swastika herself. See, e.g., http://news.bbc.co.uk/2/hi/europe/7730125.stm. Also in 2008, Julian Rees, a Jewish student at Goucher College, confessed to having etched swastikas on the inside and outside of the apartment building of another Jewish student, Shira Zemel. See, e.g., http://media.www.thequindecim.com/media/storage/paper618/news/2008/02/15/OnlineExclusives/Student.Confesses.To.Drawing.Swastika.In.Jewish.Students.Apartment-3235077.shtml.

15. ADL, "Obama's Speech to Muslim World Is 'Groundbreaking' but Misses Opportunities on the Israeli-Palestinian Conflict," 4 June 2009, available at http://www.adl.org/PresRele/IslME_62/5542_62.htm.

16. Abraham H. Foxman, "Obama in Cairo: An Error of Omission," 4 June 2009, available at http://www.adl.org/PresRele/IslME_62/Obama_Cairo_OpEd.htm.

17. Abraham H. Foxman, "Obama's Muslim Outreach: Avoiding the Pitfalls of Engagement," *Jewish Week*, 12 June 2009.

18. For scholarship disputing Israeli claims to a timeless presence in Palestine, see, e.g., Keith Whitelam, *The Invention of Ancient Israel* (London: Routledge, 1997); Nadia Abu El Haj, *Facts on the Ground* (Chicago: University of Chicago Press, 2002); and Yael Zerubavel, *Recovered Roots* (Chicago: University of Chicago Press, 1997).

19. See, e.g., Avi Shlaim, *The Iron Wall* (New York: Norton, 2001); Clayton Swisher, *The Truth about Camp David* (New York: Nation Books, 2004); Mohamed Heikal, *Secret Channels* (New York: HarperCollins, 1997); Ilan Pappe, *The Ethnic Cleansing of Palestine* (Oxford: Oneworld Publications, 2007); Rashid Khalidi, *The Iron Cage* (Boston: Beacon, 2007); and Patrick Tyler, *A World of Trouble* (New York: Farrar, Straus, and Giroux, 2008).

20. ADL, "Ford Foundation President Commits to End All Funding of Groups Linked to Incitement," 9 February 2004, available at http://www.adl.org/PresRele/ASInt_13/4448_13.htm.

21. Ibid.

22. ADL, "Anti-Semitism in Arab Media Fuels Incitement and Terrorism, ADL Tells House Foreign Affairs Committee," 22 January 2008, available at http://www.adl.org/PresRele/ASaw_14/5211_14.htm.

23. ADL, "Nazi Imagery, Anti-Semitism Rampant in Arab Media as Gaza Crisis Unfolds," 8 January 2009, available at http://www.adl.org/PresRele/ASaw_14/5435_14.htm.

24. ADL, "Israel's Operation in Gaza: Frequently Asked Questions," 22 January 2009, available at http://www.adl.org/main_Israel/FAQs_Gaza.htm.

25. Ibid.

26. Palestinian Center for Human Rights, "War on the Wounded," 13 January 2009, available at http://www.pchrgaza.org/files/Reports/English/medical5.htm.

27. PCHR, Weekly Report, 15–21 January 2009, available at http://www.pchrgaza.org/files/W_report/English/2008/22–01-2009.htm.

28. B'Tselem, "Witness Reports that Israeli Soldiers Shot Woman Waving White Flag in Gaza Strip," 13 January 2009, available at http://www.btselem.org/English/Press_Releases/20090113.asp.

29. B'Tselem, "Guidelines for Israel's Investigation into Operation Cast Lead," February 2009, pp. 4, 5, available at http://www.btselem.org/Download/200902_Operation_Cast_Lead_Position_paper_Eng.pdf.

30. Al Mezan Center for Human Rights, "The Use of Palestinian Civilians as Human Shields by the Israeli Occupation Forces," April 2009.

31. See, e.g., Chris McGreal, "Israel's Human Shields Draw Fire," *Guardian* (London), 2 January 2003; B'Tselem, "Israeli Soldiers Use Civilians as Human Shields in Beit Hanun," 20 July 2006, available at http://www.btselem.org/english/human_shields/20060720_human_shields_in_beit_hanun.asp; and "Israel 'Human Shield' Suspension," *BBC News*, 14 April 2007, available at http://news.bbc.co.uk/2/hi/middle_east/6554487.stm.

32. Sheera Frenkel and Philippe Naughton, "UN Headquarters in Gaza Hit by Israeli 'White Phosphorous' Shells," *Times* (London), 15 January 2009.

33. Robert Evans, "U.N. Reports Say Israel Targeted Civilians in Gaza," *Reuters*, 23 March 2009, available at http://www.reuters.com/article/worldNews/idUSTRE52M6G220090323.

34. David Edwards and Stephen C. Webster, "Norwegian Doctor: Israel Intentionally Targeting Civilians," *The Raw Story*, 5 January 2009, available at http://rawstory.com/news/2008/Norwegian_doctor_in_Gaza_Israel_targeting_0105.html.

35. Report of the National Lawyers Guild Delegation to Gaza, *Onslaught: Israel's Attack on Gaza and the Rule of Law*, February 2009, p. 1.

36. Chris Hedges, "A Gaza Diary," *Harper's*, October 2001, p. 64.

37. James Hider, "Israeli Soldiers Admit to Deliberate Killing of Gaza Civilians," *Times* (London), 20 March 2009.

38. Luis Ramirez, "Israeli Soldiers' Testimony on Gaza Continues to Cause Uproar," *Voice of America News*, 6 April 2009, available at http://www.voanews.com/english/Ramirez-Israel-Testimony.cfm.

39. ADL, *Fighting Extremism*, 2004, p. 3 (pamphlet).

40. This tactic has been attempted by scholar George Michael, who supposedly found a link between neo-Nazism and Muslim terrorism,

with innate hate of Israel being the primary link. The thesis didn't really catch on, however. See, e.g., George Michael, *Confronting Right Wing Extremism and Terrorism in the USA* (New York: Routledge, 2003).

41. *Fighting Extremism*, 6.

42. ADL, "American Muslim Extremists: A Growing Threat to Jews," 9 June 2009, available at http://www.adl.org/NR/exeres/D59191EC-39AF-498C-AD2C-8F40AE5A871F,DB7611A2-02CD-43AF-8147-649E26813571,frameless.htm.

43. Ibid.

44. FBI (Federal Bureau of Investigation), *Annual Threat Assessment of the Intelligence Community for the Senate Select Committee on Intelligence*, 12 February 2009, p. 7.

45. The FBI's Worldwide Incidents Tracking System is available at http://wits.nctc.gov/.

46. See, e.g., Rupert Cornwell, "Tall Stories: The Plot to Topple Chicago's Sears Tower Was Not All that It Seemed," *Independent* (London), 25 June 2006. Five of the seven suspects ended up being convicted after two mistrials.

47. See, e.g., Jennifer 8. Lee, "Fuller Portrait of Suspects in Terror Plot," *New York Times*, 22 May 2009, available at http://cityroom.blogs.nytimes.com/2009/05/22/fuller-portrait-of-suspects-in-terror-plo/.

48. See, e.g., Sunaina Maira, "Deporting Radicals, Deporting La Migra: The Hayat Case in Lodi," *Cultural Dynamics* 19, no. 1 (2007): 39–66.

49. ADL, "International Terrorist Symbols Database," available at http://www.adl.org/terrorism/symbols/default.asp.

50. Ibid.

51. Shabbas, 37.

52. Isaacs, "Spy vs Spite."

53. Ibid.

54. Committee to Defend Academic Freedom at UCSB, "Israel Lobby Descends on UC Santa Barbara," 18 May 2009, available at http://sb4af.wordpress.com/2009/05/18/israel-lobby-descends-on-uc-santa-barbara/.

55. ADL, "ADL Letter to *Santa Barbara News-Press*," 12 June 2009, available at http://www.adl.org/media_watch/newspapers/20090612-Santa+Barbara+Times.htm.

56. Silverman's letter is available at http://sb4af.files.wordpress.com/2009/04/adl_p1.jpg.

57. Committee to Defend Academic Freedom at UCSB, "UC-Santa Barbara Faculty Member Goes Public about ADL Pressure," 2 May 2009, available at http://sb4af.wordpress.com/2009/05/02/uc-santa-barbara-faculty-member-goes-public-about-adl-pressure-2/#more-474.

58. Ibid.

59. Ibid.

60. Sunaina Maira, e-mail interview with the author, 15 November 2009.

61. Isaacs, "Spy vs Spite."

62. See, e.g., Peter Balakian, *The Burning Tigris* (New York: Harper Perennial, 2004); and Taner Akcam, *A Shameful Act: The Armenian Genocide and the Question of Turkish Responsibility* (New York: Holt, 2007).

63. See, e.g., Keith O'Brien, "ADL Local Leader Fired on Armenian Issue," *Boston Globe*, 18 August 2007.

64. ADL, "ADL Statement on the Armenian Genocide," 21 August 2007, available at http://www.adl.org/PresRele/Mise_00/5114_00.htm.

65. Ibid.

66. Jennifer Siegel, "Armenian Genocide Debate Exposes Rifts at ADL," *Forward*, 24 August 2007.

67. See, e.g., http://www.adl.org/learn/ext_us/.

Chapter 3

1. Amilcar Cabral, "National Liberation and Culture," in *Colonial Discourse and Post-Colonial Theory*, ed. Patrick Williams and Laura Chrisman (New York: Columbia University Press, 1994), 54.

2. Cornel West, *Democracy Matters* (New York: Penguin, 2004), 109.

3. Ibid., 111.

4. Ibid., 115.

5. Ibid.

6. Ibid., 113.

7. See, e.g., Frank Gervasi, *The Life and Times of Menahem Begin* (New York: Putnam, 1979).

8. For a compilation of early Jewish terrorism in Palestine, see, e.g., Walid Khalidi, *Palestine Reborn* (London: I. B. Tauris, 1992).

9. See, e.g., Eugene Rogan and Avi Shlaim, eds., *The War for Palestine* (Cambridge: Cambridge University Press, 2001).

10. See, e.g., http://www.neareastconsulting.com/surveys/all/p22/out_freq_q27.php.

11. West, 110.

12. See, e.g., Nur Masalha, *Expulsion of the Palestinians* (Washington, DC: Institute for Palestine Studies, 1992).

13. West, 120.

14. Ibid., 122.

15. Ibid., 132.
16. Ibid.
17. Ibid., 142.
18. A transcript of the interview is available at http://www.democracy now.org/2008/8/29/michael_eric_dyson_puts_obamas_address.
19. Michael Eric Dyson, *Debating Race* (New York: Basic Books, 2007), 209–10.
20. Dyson writes, "Across the country, a number of black women were angry that my friend Star Jones didn't defend me against Joy Behar's charge—and in fact agreed with the assessment—that I was a racist, a charge made *after* I left the set. In light of Jones's subsequent ouster from *The View*, one can only speculate as to what, if any, role this kind of charged rhetoric may have had in her fall from grace" (ibid., 209).
21. Dyson, *Debating Race*, 202.
22. See, e.g., Robert Warrior, "Canaanites, Cowboys, and Indians: Deliverance, Conquest, and Liberation Theology Today," in *The Postmodern Bible Reader*, ed. David Jobling, Tina Pippen, and Ronald Schleifer (Oxford: Wiley-Blackwell, 2001), 188–94.
23. Dyson, *Debating Race*, 203.
24. Ibid., 203.
25. Ibid., 204.
26. Ibid., 165.
27. Ibid., 166.
28. Ibid., 181.
29. Ibid., 182–83.
30. Ibid., 183.
31. Ibid.
32. Ibid., 184.
33. Ibid.
34. Houston Baker Jr., *Betrayal* (New York: Columbia University Press, 2008), 80.
35. Ta Nehisi Coates, "The Trials of Benjamin Jealous," *The Nation*, 1 July 2009.

Chapter 4

1. Jasbir K. Puar, *Terrorist Assemblages* (Durham, NC: Duke University Press, 2007).
2. See, e.g., Gargi Bhattacharyya, *Dangerous Brown Men* (London: Zed, 2008); Chandra Talpade Mohanty, Minnie Bruce Pratt, and Robin L. Riley, *Feminism and War* (London: Zed, 2008); and Chandra Talpade

Mohanty, *Feminism Without Borders* (Durham, NC: Duke University Press, 2003).

3. The Israel Project, *Gay Rights in Israel*, 5 May 2008, available at http://www.theisraelproject.org/site/c.hsJPK0PIJpH/b.4021671/k.4F54/Gay_Rights_in_Israel.htm.

4. Ibid.

5. A synopsis of the report is available at http://www.mossawa.org/files/files/File/Reports/2009/Main%20findings%20of%20the%20Racism%20Report.pdf.

6. Yoav Stern, "Olmert: Israeli Arabs Have Long Suffered Discrimination," *Ha'aretz*, 10 December 2008.

7. Barak Ravid, "Israel Recruits Gay Community in PR Campaign against Iran," *Ha'aretz*, 20 April 2009.

8. Amal Amireh, "Israel Plans to Use Gays to Bomb Iran," *Arabisto.com*, 25 April 2009, available at http://www.arabisto.com/article/Blogs/Amal_Amireh/Israel_Plans_to_Use_Gays_to_Bomb_Iran/35281.

9. More information about the claims is available at http://www.queerty.com/shock-are-us-soldiers-responsible-for-executing-iraqs-gays-20090730/.

10. See, e.g., http://www.cnn.com/2008/WORLD/meast/07/24/gay.iraqis/.

11. A notable offender is Samantha Power, whose *A Problem from Hell* (New York: Harper Perennial, 2007) ignores genocides in which the United States is complicit and recommends American military intervention in the others.

12. James Kirchick, "Palestine and Gay Rights," *The Advocate*, 11 July 2006, available at http://www.advocate.com/exclusive_detail_ektid33587.asp.

13. Ibid.

14. Ibid.

15. http://israelity.com/category/coexistence/page/20/.

16. http://www.standwithus.com/FLYERS/images/UN%20silent poster-1.png.

17. http://www.standwithus.com/signs/pdfs/DEFENDING_ISRAEL-L_Helf.pdf.

18. http://www.standwithus.com/signs/pdfs/Skeletons.pdf.

19. My source is the organization IfAmericansKnew, which uses a strict methodology. More information is available at http://www.ifamericansknew.org/stats/children.html.

20. "Israel Minister Joins Rabbis in Opposing Tel Aviv Gay Pride," *France 24*, 10 June 2009, available at http://www.google.com/hostednews/afp/article/ALeqM5hnNAkDtj18o6CsgMR-cmuxRQWGTQ.

21. "MK Benizri: Homosexuality Causes Earthquakes," *Arutz Sheva*, 20 February 2008, available at http://www.israelnationalnews.com/News/Flash.aspx/141905.

22. Amiram Barkat, "Israel's Conservative Seminary Says No to Homosexual Students," *Ha'aretz*, 29 March 2007.

23. Alex Traiman, "Violence in Israel Caused by 'Gay' Event?" *WorldNetDaily*, 19 July 2006, available at http://www.wnd.com/news/article.asp?ARTICLE_ID=51128.

24. See, e.g., Ahiya Raved, "Haifa Gays: Police Ignore Us," *Yediot Ahronot*, 4 August 2009, available at http://www.ynetnews.com/articles/0,7340,L-3757204,00.html.

25. See, e.g., John-Henry Westen, "Gay 'Marriage' in Israel: Worse than Holocaust—Will Cause Terrorism, Warns Rabbi," *LifeSiteNews*, 21 November 2006, http://www.lifesitenews.com/ldn/2006/nov/06112107.html.

26. See, e.g., Edward Said, *Orientalism* (New York: Vintage, 1979).

27. Joseph Massad, *Desiring Arabs* (Chicago: University of Chicago Press, 2007), 9.

28. Ibid., 37, emphasis his.

29. Kathryn Babayan and Afsaneh Najmabadi, eds., *Islamicate Sexualities* (Cambridge: Harvard Middle Eastern Monographs, 2008).

30. Khaled El-Rouayheb, *Before Homosexuality in the Arab-Islamic World, 1500–1800* (Chicago: University of Chicago Press, 2005), 5.

31. Ibid., 1.

32. I deem *Bruno* exploitative for the same reason that I find problems with the funnier character Borat, the protagonist of the eponymous 2006 film. While Bruno and Borat purport to expose tacit attitudes of discrimination, and often do a fine job of it, it is difficult to forgive Baron Cohen for misleading a Romanian village and underpaying its residents. It's equally difficult to forgive his misrepresentation of an innocent Palestinian, Ayman Abu Aita, as a terrorist, especially when Baron Cohen is earning millions for his antics while his bamboozled targets earn nothing but scorn and ridicule. The line between edgy satire and exploitation can often be thin; Baron Cohen clearly exists on the side of exploitation. In both *Borat* and *Bruno*, he reifies the same stereotypes he sets out to expose in others.

33. Rachel Shabi, "The Non-Profit Worker from Bethlehem Who Was Branded a Terrorist by Bruno," *Guardian* (London), 31 July 2009.

34. Aaron Klein, " 'Terrorist Leader' Threatens to Sue 'Bruno' Movie," *WorldNetDaily*, 12 July 2009, available at http://www.wnd.com/index.php?fa=PAGE.view&pageId=103797.

35. Jasbir K. Puar, *Terrorist Assemblages*, 16–17.

36. Ibid., xiii.

37. Ibid., 4.
38. Ibid., 17.
39. Nathan Jeffay, "Waving Israel's Rainbow Flag Abroad," *Forward*, 26 June 2009.
40. Ibid.
41. Ofri Ilani, "Haaretz Survey: 46% of Israelis Think Gays Are Deviants," *Ha'aretz*, 8 June 2009, available at http://haaretz.com/hasen/spages/1105652.html.

Chapter 5

1. Chinua Achebe, *Hopes and Impediments* (New York: Anchor, 1989), 2–3.
2. See, e.g., Kameel B. Nasr, *Arab and Israeli Terrorism: The Causes and Effects of Political Violence* (Jefferson, NC: McFarland, 2007); see also As'ad Abukhalil, "Spielberg on Munich," available at http://angryarab.blogspot.com/2005/12/spielberg-on-munich-humanization-of.html.
3. See, e.g., Robert Fisk, *Pity the Nation: Lebanon at War*, 3rd ed. (Oxford: Oxford University Press, 2001); and Bayan Nuwayhed al-Hout, *Sabra and Shatila: September 1982* (London: Pluto Books, 2004).
4. Kelly Hartog, "Filmmaker Reveals 'Waltz with Bashir' Backstory," *Jewish Telegraphic Agency*, 13 January 2009, available at http://jta.org/news/article/2009/01/13/1002224/filmmaker-reveals-waltz-with-bashir-backstory.
5. Ibid.
6. Brad Balfour, "An Israeli Director Dances with the Dogs of War in *Waltz with Bashir*," *Pop Entertainment*, 1 March 2009, http://www.popentertainment.com/folman.htm.
7. Jonathan Freedland, "Lest We Forget," *Guardian* (London), 25 October 2008.
8. See, e.g., Ze'ev Schiff and Ehud Ya'ari, *Israel's Lebanon War* (New York: Touchstone, 1985).
9. In addition to numerous historians and social critics, the UN deemed Sabra and Shatila an act of genocide in Resolution 37/123D, whose text is available at http://www.un.org/documents/ga/res/37/a37r123.htm.
10. The passage is taken from a brief introduction to the report, which is available in its entirety at http://www.jewishvirtuallibrary.org/jsource/History/kahan.html.
11. Begin's statement is in a January 1983 *Time* magazine article, available at http://www.time.com/time/magazine/article/0,9171,953639,00.html.

12. It turns out that the murder wasn't the work of Palestinians but of a disgruntled Lebanese Orthodox Christian, Habib Shartouni, who was allied with Syria and angry because of Gemayel's close relationship with Israel. See, e.g., Ze'ev Schiff, *Israel's Lebanon War* (New York: Touchstone, 1985), 247.

Index

Steven Salaita is associate professor of English at Virginia Tech. His recent books include *The Uncultured Wars*, *Anti-Arab Racism in the USA*, and *The Holy Land in Transit*.